THE COMPLEAT TRAVELER'S COMPANION

Country New England Inns

by

Anthony Hitchcock

and

Jean Lindgren

ARTEMIS BOOKS

© 1978 by Burt Franklin & Co., Inc.

Published by Artemis Books
235 East Forty-fourth Street
New York, New York 10017

Library of Congress Cataloging in Publication Data

Hitchcock, Anthony, 1940–
Country New England inns.

(The Compleat traveler's companion)
1. Hotels, taverns, etc. — New England —
Directories.   I. Lindgren, Jean, 1941–   joint author.
II. Title.   III. Series.
TX907.H55   647′.9574   78-6379
ISBN 0-89102-139-6
ISBN 0-89102-135-3 pbk.

Designed by Bernard Schleifer

Printed in the United States of America

Contents

Introduction

PEOPLE ARE DRAWN to New England for many reasons. Some are attracted by its long coastline with its variety of beaches. Others love the inland areas with their myriad of lakes, forests, rolling hills, and mountains. Sportsmen enjoy New England year round for its hunting, fishing, boating, skiing, swimming, mountain climbing, or hiking. Artists come to paint; writers come to write. Theatre lovers come for summer theatre, and history buffs come to observe the lessons of the past represented in the thousands of museums, historical societies, and historic sites that are found in every corner of the states. For our part, we find ourselves drawn back by some even more deeply rooted force, perhaps from our childhood. One of us was born and spent the better part of his youth in New England, and the other has summered there for many years. For whatever reason and in whatever season, you will find New England a most compelling place. It is unlikely that you will fail to return. Many never leave.

If you have decided to go, here are some helpful suggestions. First, choose your season and area with care. If you cannot cope with snow, you will certainly know not to select a winter weekend. It is not so well known, however, that the early-spring mud season makes travel on back roads in the three most northerly states trying at best. If you plan an April trip to a remote inn, be sure to ask if local travel will be a problem.

We also suggest you write early for literature about inns that you have chosen as interesting. Read the brochures, look at the pictures, check the maps, and determine if the inns will actually meet your needs. Inns are not like motels at all. Each has special qualities that can be one's personal pleasure, but not necessarily another's. Do not hesitate to call an innkeeper and discuss your requirements. Most innkeepers are highly understanding of the needs of their clients. If you are seeking an old-fashioned small country inn that is secluded, with few outside distractions, then ask before you go. We have purposely included a range of inns, from the simplest to small resorts.

We also point out that the quoted rates at all inns described in this book are subject to change. Be sure to ask what the current rates are and what they include. Many inns automatically add a service charge of from 10 to 20 percent that covers all gratuities. The more expensive rooms are the ones with the best views, fireplaces, or other special features that you may or may not want. If your room is described as having a fireplace, be sure to ask if it may actually be used; some are merely decorative. If you have a working fireplace, ask if wood is included in the room rate. One inn we stayed at (and did not include here) charged us extra for the fireplace and then added two charges for wood delivered to our door. We had forgotten to ask in advance.

We also suggest you ask if your room rate includes meals. We have listed room rates as being based on no meals, the American Plan (AP; all three meals included), or the Modified American Plan (MAP; breakfast and dinner included). Some inns use the term European Plan (EP) to mean no meals included, and some use it to indicate that a continental breakfast of rolls and coffee or tea is included. We prefer this last plan, which frees us to explore a region's restaurants. The various American plans may seem constraining to some, but in very rural areas they may turn out to be the only possible option.

A wealth of travel information can be obtained free of charge from the highly organized state and local chambers of commerce as well as several promotional organizations serving the New England area. One of the best sources is the *New England Council*. The Council operates visitors' centers in several states where tourists can gather armloads of pamphlets describing places to stay, recreational facilities, and historic sites to visit. The Council's headquarters is at 1032 Statler Office Building, Boston, Mass. 02116. Phone: 617-542-2580. The New York City office of the Council is located at 1268 Avenue of the Americas, New York, N.Y. 10020. Phone: 212-757-4455. Both centers maintain a ski-report service in the winter.

The single best source of state information in a compact form is found on the back of the official road map for each state. These are issued by the respective state departments of transportation, but may be obtained from the individual state departments of commerce and development. All these departments offer extensive vacation-planning material in addition to the maps and will be glad to steer you

4

to individual areas' chambers of commerce, which are listed in this volume in the introductions to the individual states.

For the convenience of readers, this book is organized by state, and into regional subsections within most states. Within the regional subsections, the listings are alphabetical by the names of towns and villages, *not* by the names of the inns. Throughout the introductions to the villages, readers will note that points of interest appear printed in italics. This is to indicate that the particular attraction is described in detail in one of the three companion volumes in this series: Country New England Sightseeing and Historical Guide, Country New England Sports and Recreation, and Country New England Antiques, Crafts, and Factory Outlets. Described in those three books are hundreds and hundreds of things to do and places to see throughout the entire New England area.

And finally, the inns described in this book were chosen for their inherent charm, based partially on their architectural style, location, furnishings, and history. The information incorporated here came from several sources: our personal knowledge of inns, recommendations of others we deem reliable, and personal surveys of innkeepers. We have made every effort to provide information as carefully and accurately as possible, but we remind readers again that all rates and schedules listed are subject to change. Further, we have neither solicited nor accepted any fees or gratuities for inclusion in this book or any of the other books in this series. Should readers wish to suggest corrections for future editions or offer their own comments, we welcome their correspondence. Please write to us in care of our publishers, Artemis Books, 235 East 44th Street, New York, N.Y., 10017.

Have a good trip.

Anthony Hitchcock
Jean Lindgren

Connecticut

CONNECTICUT WAS frequently explored by trading parties dispatched from the Dutch trading colony based on the island of Manhattan. The first permanent settlement consisted of Puritans who had left Massachusetts under the leadership of Reverend Thomas Hooker in the year 1633. In 1639, the "Fundamental Orders" were written. Most historians believe this document to be the world's first written constitution, outlining as it did the basic form of democratic government that was to prevail within the state. The publication of this important document lead to Connecticut's being called the "Constitution State." Connecticut sent many of its finest men to fight the British in the American Revolution. One of them, General Israel Putnam, shouted the now famous "Don't shoot until you see the whites of their eyes" at the battle of Bunker Hill. Other well-known Connecticut citizens who contributed to the American effort during the revolution were Nathan Hale and Governor John Trumbull, and Benedict Arnold, before he went over to the British.

During the nineteenth and twentieth centuries the tremendous expansion of trade industrialized the Connecticut coastline communities from Norwalk to New Haven and along much of the Connecticut River. Much of interior Connecticut, however, remains surprisingly rural and draws a tourist population in all four seasons, as do many coastal villages.

To obtain useful travel information, contact the State Department of Tourism at the following address: Connecticut Department of Commerce, Division of Tourism, 210 Washington Street, Hartford, CT 06100. The telephone number is 203-566-3977. One particularly helpful publication is "Connecticut, So Much, So Near."

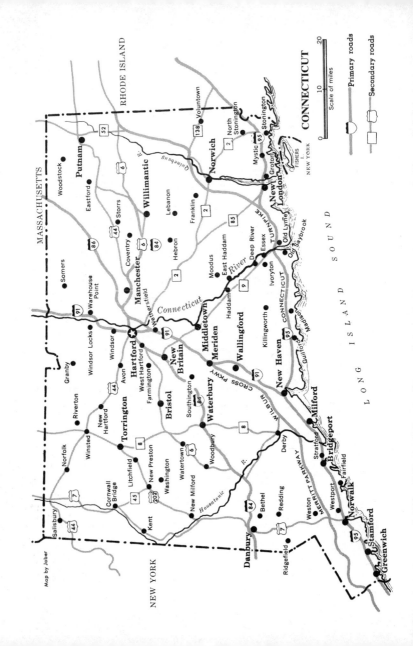

WESTERN

Greenwich, Connecticut

Greenwich is one of the oldest settlements in Connecticut, dating from 1640 when it was purchased from the Miossehassaky Indian tribe by two agents of the New Haven colony who named it after Greenwich, England. These agents were not the first Europeans to set foot in the area; a regiment of explorers headed by Captain Adrian Block—for whom Block Island was later named—had stopped in what is now Greenwich in 1614 while on an exploratory mission out of the Dutch trading settlement on Manhattan Island.

Today Greenwich, just 30 miles from Manhattan, has a population of 63,200 and contains several important places of interest. *Putnam Cottage* is a prerevolutionary house maintained by the DAR and open to the public. The *Bush Holly House* is the headquarters of the Greenwich Historical Society; it houses the Society's museum and a fine display of antique farm tools and household utensils. Also in Greenwich is the *Museum of Cartoon Art* and the *Bruce Museum*, with its displays in the areas of natural history, physical science, and American Indian studies. The National Audubon Society is particularly proud of the *Audubon Center* with its 447-acre nature preserve, noted for an abundance of wild flowers and an excellent self-guiding nature trail.

THE HOMESTEAD INN

420 Field Point Road, Greenwich CT 06830. 203-869-7500. *Innkeeper:* Cal Estes. Open all year. Lunch and dinner served daily except Sunday in dining room.

The Homestead Inn, situated on a hill that overlooks Greenwich, has 25 guest rooms. The main part was built in 1799 and the dining room was added in 1859. The building has been carefully restored by its present owner. A wide, sweeping veranda, complete with wicker and lounge chairs, gives the inn a Victorian air.

The inn is decorated with period antiques. Each room is different, but all have modern conveniences such as private bath and

television. There is a fireplace in the parlor to warm guests in winter. Outside are many old shade trees on wide lawns. Summer guests can enjoy lunch served at poolside.

The dining room menu is varied, offering such choices as fresh Bay of Fundy scallops, roast duckling with an unusual burgundy black cherry sauce, and peppermint black bottom pie. *Room Rates*: Single rooms, $22 and up; double rooms, $24 to $30; suites, $36 to $40. There is a $3-a-day charge for pets. Reservations are required, and should be made well in advance during summer months. *Driving Instructions*: Three minutes from Greenwich. Take I-95 to exit 3. Turn left at railroad bridge and go two blocks to end. Turn left again and proceed ¼ mile up hill to the inn.

Litchfield, Connecticut

Litchfield was purchased from the Tunxis Indians for 15 pounds sterling in 1716 and incorporated by the Connecticut Colonial Assembly in 1719. The land was formally settled by a group of 60 families the next year. During the American Revolution, Litchfield was a major supplier of cannons and munitions made in its several foundries. For years the town was an important stagecoach stop for both the Albany-New Haven and the Boston-Hartford lines. Industry never developed in Litchfield, as it did in the many mill towns of New England, because it is located at too high an elevation to have any useful source of water power that was so abundantly available to towns in the river valleys. Today, the quiet village has a population of only 7500, less than double the population of 1810.

Litchfield is one of the best-preserved examples of an eighteenth-century village in America, largely *because* it was bypassed by the Industrial Revolution. The town offers a number of tourist attractions including the *Litchfield Law School*, the first such school in America, where Tapping Reeve taught law to, among others, Aaron Burr in 1775. More than 1000 pupils passed through this school, including two vice-presidents of the United States. The *Litchfield Historical Society* contains four galleries of art and historical artifacts, as well as a "Please Do Touch" exhibit for children. Also in Litchfield is the *White Memorial Foundation*, its 4000 acres open for public recreation with facilities for swimming, fishing, boating, hiking, cross-country skiing, snowshoeing, and more. Part of the grounds are devoted to the *Litchfield Nature Center and Museum* with its wildlife dioramas, nature trails, and special *Braille Nature Trail*.

THE MEETINGHOUSE INN

West Street (Route 202), Litchfield, CT 06759. 203-567-8744. *Innkeeper*: Denise Sherwood; owners: Mr. and Mrs. Raymond Sass, Jr. Open all year, except Christmas day.

The Meetinghouse Inn was constructed in 1760 high atop a hill in historic Litchfield. Originally a farmhouse, it has undergone many renovations—one such by Col. Albert Lamb in 1900. He turned the inn into the magnificent Georgian colonial building it is today. The Meetinghouse is set off by its four acres of manicured grounds, gardens, flowering shrubs, and old shade trees. Nine colorful guest rooms are available to travelers. All rooms are uniquely decorated, each with a private bath; some also have fireplaces. There are three distinctly different dining rooms and a "Taproom" with an enormous copper bar. The two main dining rooms contain antique-filled cupboards, chandeliers, period prints, and fireplaces. Overlooking the tree-shaded lawns and terrace, the glassed-in "Porch" filled with hanging plants offers a third dining area.

The inn features both traditional New England fare and continental cuisine. The specialties are coquilles St. Jacques, prime

11

ribs, and veal a la Oscar, a sautéed cutlet topped with asparagus spears, crabmeat and Béarnaise sauce. *Room Rates*: Single rooms, $35 to $40; double rooms, $40 to $45; suite, $75. Reservations are suggested from spring to fall. Pets are permitted. *Driving Instructions*: 9/10 mile west from the Litchfield green on Route 202.

New Preston, Connecticut

New Preston is located on Lake Waramaug, one of the biggest and most beautiful lakes in the state. It is surrounded by the foothills of the Berkshires, with their mountains and hills dropping down to its shores. Biking, hiking, or driving around the lake is a memorable experience. The back roads of New Preston abound with colonial homes and well-kept farms. Water mills and covered bridges dot the area. During the Revolutionary War this area's many ironworks in the water-powered mills manufactured cannons and arms for the American troops.

The lake provides year-round sports activities, including fishing, skating, and boating. For spectators, there is the *Eastern Women's Sprints Regatta* (crew racing) in May. Antique carriage rallies, marathons, fairs, and auctions are just some of the varied entertainments the area around New Preston and Lake Waramaug have to offer the visitor.

BOULDERS INN

Route 45, New Preston, CT 06777. 203-868-7918. *Innkeepers*: Mr. and Mrs. Richard Lowe; manager: Peter Franklin. Open

12

from May 15 through October, with full service and meals available; from November 1 through May 15, rooms and breakfast only. Closed Christmas.

Up in the Berkshire hills on 230 acres of woods and lake frontage sits Boulders Inn. Built in 1895, the inn has been run by the Lowe family for four generations. The main house is constructed of huge fieldstones with granite lintels. Large windows overlook Lake Waramaug and the surrounding hills. About 500 feet of private shore provides excellent swimming with a sandy, gentle slope for children and a deep-water float for swimmers. The waters are well stocked for guests who want to fish and there are also boating, sailing, and canoeing available. Riding stables offer scenic trails and instruction. The property includes a large barn with an open fireplace, lounges, a snack bar, and games. In warm weather, the big old doors open onto a terrace where weekly cookouts are held, and traditional barn dances are a regular feature in the 60-foot structure.

In winter, Boulders has a toboggan run and ski slope with a 500-foot tow. Snowshoers and cross-country skiers blaze the snowy trails for hikers. For those who love the outdoors, the lake and pond provide ice skating and ice fishing; other guests prefer to relax by the crackling hearth and enjoy the winter scenery.

The main building contains a blend of antiques and comfortable furniture. The inn's bedrooms have views of the lake and the countryside. Six spacious rooms have private baths, antique furnishings, and new beds. In addition, there are several cottages on the property. The Boulders cottages are modern, and some have kitchenettes. The valley cottages, located in a secluded setting a five-minute walk from the inn, are rustic and casual. *Room Rates:* There are various plans with or without meals; prices (American plan) range from approximately $22 to $35 per person. Pets are permitted in the off season (November 1–May 15) only. *Driving Instructions:* Take Rt. 84 to exit 7, then Rt. 7 to New Milford. Take Rt. 202 to New Preston. Left on Rt. 45 to Lake Waramaug and the inn.

HOPKINS INN

Hopkins Road, New Preston, CT 06777. 203-868-7295. *Innkeepers*: Beth and Franz Schober. Open from May through October; meals available April to January, except on Mondays.

The Hopkins Inn, also on Lake Waramaug, was built in 1846, although the barn section predates the main house. The inn was owned and operated continuously by members of the Hopkins family for over 100 years (until 1954). There is a terrace for outdoor warm-weather dining overlooking the lake. The cuisine is mostly continental, and diners may choose from the 10 to 15 items which are listed daily on the dining room blackboard. Both luncheon and dinner are offered to the public, but breakfast is available to inn guests only. *Room Rates:* Double rooms with private bath, $20 to $23. Pets are permitted, within reason. *Driving Instructions:* The inn is ½ mile west of Route 45 on North Shore Road.

THE INN ON LAKE WARAMAUG

Lake Shore Road, New Preston, CT 06777. 203-868-2168. *Innkeeper:* Richard Bonynge Combs. Open all year.

The Inn on Lake Waramaug also sits on a hill, surrounded by sloping lawns and fields and towering sugar maples, overlooking Connecticut's second largest natural lake. Built between 1795 and 1815, it has operated as an inn and tavern since 1860. The main building is furnished with pine and cherry antiques, and houses collections of pewter, brass, and copper. Daguerreotypes, cupboards filled with lace fans, and silver tea services add to the atmosphere of the inn. With the addition of several new colonial-styled guest buildings, an indoor heated swimming pool, and porches and terraces on the old building itself, the inn has become a family resort. Nowhere is this resort atmosphere more evident than in the pool building with its whirlpool lagoon, sauna, snack

14

bar, barefoot bar, and a connecting game room. There is a tennis court with professional lessons available in the summer months, as well as volleyball, badminton, and croquet. Guests can have free, unlimited golf at a nearby club.

Though the inn may appeal more to the activity-minded than to those seeking a small, quiet country place, one can certainly stay at one of the inn's rooms dating from the 1800s and also enjoy the amenities of the resort, such as the recently added summer cart rides and winter sleigh rides with the vehicles drawn by Chester, Happy, and Merrylegs—the inn's ponies. The inn also sponsors numerous events throughout the year including wine-tasting evenings, family picnics on the beach, Wednesday night bingo, a Fourth of July clambake, and much more. *Room Rates*: July, August, weekends, and holiday weeks, double rooms, $33 per person, MAP. Rates for the remainder of the year, $30 per person. Single occupancy rates are higher. European plan is available at certain times and under certain conditions. Write or phone the inn for information. Pets are permitted. *Driving Instructions*: The inn is located in northwest Connecticut off Route 202 between New Milford and Litchfield. Take Route 45 to the north end of Lake Waramaug. Turn left onto Lake Shore Road. The inn is about ¾ mile down the road.

Norwalk (and neighboring New Canaan)

Norwalk, a city with a population of 77,000, is located in southern Connecticut between Stamford and Bridgeport. The city has always been an important industrial area and now is a suburban center as well. The Silvermine area, which derived its name from an early settler who falsely believed that he had discovered silver there, has retained its country feeling.

Norwalk itself boasts the *Lockwood-Mathews Mansion* which is open on a limited basis to the public while the grand building is restored to its former condition. The *Silvermine Guild of Artists* in nearby New Canaan has several galleries open all year; it sometimes sponsors special art shows. *Old MacDonald's Farm* on Route 1 in Norwalk is an eight-acre amusement part with tame animals and other entertainments for children. Nearby New Canaan is also the home of the *New Canaan Bird Sanctuary and Wildlife Preserve* with its 18 acres of trails, bridges, and ponds. *The New Canaan Nature Center* has a number of nature displays and greenhouse exhibits. The *New Canaan Historical Society* maintains several old buildings housing museums which display such things as antique pewter, tools, costumes, and the work of John Rodgers, a nineteenth-century sculptor.

SILVERMINE TAVERN

Perry Avenue and Silvermine Avenue, Norwalk, CT 06850. 20-3-847-4558. *Innkeeper*: Francis Whitman. Open all year, but closed Tuesdays in winter.

Four buildings comprise the Tavern group—the Coach House, the Old Mill, the Country Store, and the Tavern itself. The buildings are furnished with antiques, Oriental rugs, and primitive paintings. Each guest room has its own private bath and authentic antique beds (three with canopies). Several rooms have balconies overlooking the millpond. A waterfall contributes to the charm of the 200-year-old building, The Old Mill; crackling fireplaces in winter, leafy shade trees in summer, and colorful foliage in autumn all create an atmosphere of warm New England hospitality.

The Tavern has several dining rooms overlooking the swans on the millpond and the wooded banks of the Silvermine River. It is decorated with unusual kitchen utensils and primitive portraits, and it is very popular with tourists. The menu features traditional New England fare, shore dinners, Boston scrod, steaks, and chicken. The Tavern is particularly proud of its Indian pudding.

Room Rates: Single rooms, $16 to $18 plus tax; double rooms, $27 to $30 plus tax. Reservations are advised year-round. Pets are permitted and are the owners' responsibility. *Driving Instructions*: Exit 39 on Merritt Parkway (Route 15). Proceed south on Route 7 to the first traffic light, then turn right on Perry Avenue. Follow for 1½ miles to the inn.

Old Saybrook, Connecticut

The first Europeans to visit the Old Saybrook area were lead in 1614 by the Dutch explorer Adrian Block, a representative of the Dutch trading colony in what is now Manhattan. Block returned to the Connecticut River many times on trading voyages but no settlement by Europeans was made until 1636, when a fort was built by Lion Gardiner (later of Gardiner's Island, New York). The original patents which granted rights to settle this land were given by King James I to the Earl of Warwick, who then formed a syndicate to colonize his holdings. The heads of the syndicate were Viscounts Saye and Sele and Lord Brooks; it is from these men that the name of the town was taken. The first submarine ever used in combat was built in Old Saybrook in 1775 by the inventor, David Bushnell. It was a wooden craft whose lone occupant turned the propeller by hand.

Today, Old Saybrook is a town of 9200 people. The area has fine boating in both the Connecticut River and the Long Island Sound and there are several marinas and a *Town Beach*. The annual *Outdoor Art Show* is held the last weekend in July. The *Old Saybrook Historical Society* maintains a small museum.

CASTLE INN AT CORNFIELD POINT

Hartland Drive, Old Saybrook, CT 06475. 203-388-4681. *Innkeepers*: David Garfield, Ron MacDaniel, and Fred Lucia. Open all year.

The Castle Inn, a 38-room stone mansion, is situated on a cliff overlooking the Long Island Sound. Built at the turn of the century as a private residence, the inn was recently purchased by Garfield, MacDaniel, and Lucia. They have launched a major renovation project and the building is now well on its way to recap-

17

turing its former elegance. The big public rooms are wainscoted, and stained-glass windows have been added to the lounges and dining room. The main rooms are furnished with Victorian antiques. When we called, the guest rooms had not yet been redone and were still furnished in "motel modern" but their restoration is definitely scheduled for the near future. The second- and third-floor rooms enjoy a scenic view of the water. The mansion is constructed of massive beach-stone walls, with some exposed in the inn's dining room. The extensive menu features local seafood, beef, and a variety of coffees, including Jamaican, Irish, French, and Italian espresso. The restaurant is open to the public and serves a Sunday buffet brunch from 11 A.M. to 2:30 P.M.

A 70-foot pool is available for guests' use in summer. Within walking distance there are two beaches, tennis, golf, and boating. *Room Rates*: Double rooms, $28 upstairs, $23 downstairs. Reservations required except in winter. No pets permitted. *Driving Instructions*: Main Street Saybrook to Maple Avenue, then right to stop. Take left to first right, then follow road to inn.

Ridgefield, Connecticut

Settled in 1709, Ridgefield is a charming colonial town. Old houses line the tree-shaded Main Street. *Keeler Tavern*, also known as The Cannon Ball House because of a ball still buried in a corner post, is located on Main Street. The tavern, which has a fine collection of antique furnishings, sells jams, preserves, and craft items in its shop. Also on Main Street is the *Aldrich Museum of Con-*

temporary Art, with its sculpture garden. Ridgefield has an annual Antique Car Rally and Show in September.

STONEHENGE
Route 7, Ridgefield, CT 06877. 203-438-6511. *Innkeepers*: David Davis and Douglas Seville. Open all year.

Stonehenge is a large white brick and fieldstone farmhouse which was built in 1832. Swans, Canadian geese, and mallards glide on the lily-covered trout pond. The inn is surrounded by 10 acres of lawns and big shade trees. There are two large guest rooms with fireplaces in the farmhouse and six rooms in the shady annex; all are furnished with antiques.

Known for its splendid cuisine, Stonehenge serves unusual food at breakfast, lunch, and dinner. Appetizers include their own smoked sausage with mustard wine sauce, smoked trout, and shrimp in beer batter with a pungent fruit sauce. Main course specialties include fresh brook trout, roast rack of lamb, pheasant and venison in season, and (given five days notice) roast suckling pig. Only 1¼ hours from New York City, a weekend at Stonehenge is a quiet, restful way to enjoy haute cuisine. *Room Rates*: $35 to $45. Reservations are required. No pets permitted. *Driving Instructions*: Off Route 7 in Ridgefield.

Salisbury, Connecticut
Salisbury is a small village in the far northwestern corner of Connecticut, a most attractive place to explore. Nearby is Mount Riga State Park and the northernmost part of the Housatonic State Forest. Salisbury is a short drive from the Massachusetts Berkshires with their skiing and points of historical interest.

WHITE HART INN
Junction, Routes 41 and 44, Salisbury, CT 06068. 203-435-2511. *Innkeeper*: John D. Harney. Open all year.

Located on the village green in Salisbury, the White Hart Inn was built in 1800 as a private residence, but has been in continuous service as a hostelry since 1867. The inn is actually a three-building complex consisting of the original 1800 building, an adjacent

annex that was also built as a residence, and at one time served as a private girls' school, and a more modern seven-room motor-court-type building next to the inn. Guests, therefore, have a choice of accommodations in several styles. All rooms are comfortable and have private baths and telephones. Ten of the inn rooms are air conditioned.

The inn employs an Oriental chef, so the menu has an interesting combination of Oriental, continental, and American cuisine. Among the many dishes offered are Buddha's ten ingredient vegetables, sliced pork with oyster sauce, mixed meats in hot spicy sauce, shrimp with cashews, tea smoked flavor duckling, rainbow trout Bretonne, tournedos of beef Bordelaise, and broiled filet mignon. These are only a small sample of the 32 different entrees available, ranging in price from $5.95 to $9.95.

The inn maintains an old-fashioned country store within the main building, complete with potbelly stove and bayberry candles. Also available for sale are old lamps, maple sugar, cheddar cheese, and more. *Room Rates*: All rooms are European Plan. In inn and annex, single rooms, $16 to $20; double rooms, $18.50 to $24.50. Motel rooms are $2 to $4 additional. Reservations are required on weekends. Pets are permitted. *Driving Instructions*: The inn is located on the village green at the junctions of Routes 44 and 41.

Woodbury, Connecticut

Woodbury is a lovely old New England town with a large number of houses that predate 1750 and that have been restored to their original state. Among several points of interest is the *Glebe House*,

birthplace of the American Episcopacy and site of Samuel Sea-
bury's election as the first bishop of the Episcopal Church in
America. Part of this building has been restored to represent a
home of the period in which it was built (1740) and part is a
church museum. Also in Woodbury is the *Flanders Nature Center*,
an 830-acre sanctuary with walking trails and special environmental
displays. The town has a number of excellent antique shops. It is a
short drive from another New England village, Litchfield (described earlier).

THE CURTIS HOUSE

506 Main Street, Woodbury, CT 06798. 203-263-2101. *Innkeeper*: Garwin Hardisty. Open all year. Restaurant is closed
Christmas Day only.

The Curtis House first opened its doors in 1754, and has been in
continuous operation ever since. It now claims to be the oldest inn
in the state. The main house has eight rooms with private baths
and fourposter canopied beds. Six other rooms share a common
bath, and are furnished with period antiques "wherever practical."
On wintry evenings, cheery fireplaces blaze in the public room.

The dining room is open to the public. It serves lunch and dinner featuring a large seafood selection and a flaky chicken pot pie.
In the mornings, coffee, toast, and juice are served to guests.

For a vacation or a weekend stay, such activities as swimming,
boating, and horseback riding are available nearby. The town of
Woodbury also has some 30 antique shops for browsing or buying.
Room Rates: Without private bath, single rooms, $8; double
rooms, $12. With private bath, singles, $12 to $15; doubles, $18 to
$20. Tax is additional. Reservations are recommended. No pets
permitted. *Driving Instructions*: Route 6 to Woodbury; inn is 1000
yards on the left.

EASTERN

Eastford, Connecticut

Eastford is a tiny village (population 900) in north central
Connecticut. The village is most noted for the success story of Al-

bert Buell who started a small gloxinia business with a few leaf cuttings and a packet of seeds in 1944. Today *Buell Greenhouses* is one of the country's major growers of both gloxinias and African violets, with sales in excess of 300,000 plants annually. Within driving distance of the town is the University of Connecticut at Storrs with its Jorgensen Center for theater and music. *Caprilands Herb Garden* is in nearby Coventry. Here Adelma Simmons presides over a thriving herb business and serves luncheons featuring talks on herbs along with herb-accented meals. The Eastford area provides a variety of opportunities for cross-country skiing in the winter and hiking or exploring back roads in the warmer months.

GENERAL LYON INN

Route 198, Eastford, CT 06242. 203-947-1380. *Innkeepers*: John and Dorothy Bowen. Open all year.

The General Lyon was the first New England inn we visited a number of years ago and it has retained every bit of its charm during our many return visits. To arrive at Eastford and the General Lyon is to step back into the days when stagecoaches stopped there on the Boston to Hartford run. The inn, which shared its beginning with the nation's in 1776, was renamed for General Nathaniel Lyon, an Eastford resident killed in the Civil War. His funeral was attended by 14,000 people including members of Lincoln's cabinet, who stayed at the inn.

The inn is now furnished in eighteenth- and nineteenth-century antiques which give it a genuinely old feeling. The bedrooms are simple and all share bath facilities. No attempt has been made to modernize unnecessarily.

Meals at the General Lyon are an example of true Yankee cooking at its best—perfectly done pot roast, roast lamb, or baked stuffed flounder. All gravies, breads, and desserts are homemade; the breads, in fact, are still baked in the old ovens.

The General Lyon will appeal to any traveler who enjoys simple, quiet country lodging and food. The inn operates a small antique shop in an adjacent building with a selection of well-priced American antiques. *Room Rates*: Single rooms, $12; double rooms, $16. Reservations are required. Pets not permitted. *Driving Instructions*: Take Route 44 to Phoenixville and turn north on Route 198 to Eastford and the inn.

Ivoryton, Connecticut

Ivoryton was once New England's center for the ivory trade, from which the town derived its name. Elephant tusks, shipped from far-off Zanzibar, were transformed into organ and piano keys in the local factories. The Pratt Read Company is still in operation today, although they now discourage the use of ivory. The village is the home of the *Ivoryton Playhouse* on Main Street, a summer theater.

There is much to do in the surrounding area. A few miles to the north, on the Connecticut River, is the town of Haddam with its now famous *Goodspeed Opera House* where such Broadway musicals as *Man of La Mancha* and *Annie* were born. Farther up the river and on the opposite bank is the *Gillette Castle* and State Park. At the river's mouth is Old Saybrook with its many antique stores and its annual sidewalk art display, held in late July. A comfortable drive away is *Mystic Seaport*, east of New London.

COPPER BEECH INN

Main Street, Ivoryton, CT 06442. 203-767-0330. *Innkeepers*: Mr. and Mrs. Robert McKenzie. Open all year.

The Copper Beech Inn has a renowned restaurant which has been awarded four stars by the Mobil Guide and has been praised by restaurant reviewers from nearly all the major magazines and newspapers that cover the central Connecticut region. Few people know that the inn also contains five guest rooms.

This Victorian mansion, dating from 1898, has gained its reputation for an extensive menu, which can best be described as country French classic. Diners are served in any of four well-appointed di-

ning rooms, furnished with Queen Anne and Chippendale antiques and decorated with old paintings and prints. One dining room is actually the mansion's former greenhouse, which has been converted into a four-season eating place by the careful treatment of the glass to reject unwanted heat in the warmer months. Diners can choose from a selection of foods that includes 19 appetizers, 4 soups, 19 entrees, and 3 sandwich-salad combinations. Entrees are served with fresh vegetables, salad, and a small loaf of French bread. The dessert menu lists 21 items. There is also a well thought out seven-page wine list which includes offerings ranging in price from $5.50 to $150 (for a 1949 Chateau Latour Pauillac) per bottle.

The inn's five double rooms contain their original cast iron bathtubs in their private baths. *Room Rates*: $32.10. No pets permitted. *Driving Instructions*: From Hartford, take 91 south to Route 9 south, exit 4. Turn right at end of exit, and right again at the light. The inn is 1¼ miles further on the left. From New London or New Haven, take 95 to exit 69 (Route 9N). Take that to exit 3 and turn left. The inn is 2½ miles further on the left.

Old Lyme, Connecticut

Old Lyme is currently a summer art colony and home of the *Lyme Art Association* with its year-round gallery and special Art Association shows held annually from Memorial Day weekend through mid-June, late June through July, and early August through mid-September. The *Florence Griswold House*, built in 1817, is a Georgian mansion housing a collection of paintings and murals by members of America's oldest artist colony as well as antiques, toys, dolls, and rare china.

BEE AND THISTLE INN

100 Lyme Street, Old Lyme, CT 06371. 203-434-1667. Open all year.

The Bee and Thistle is a quiet, relaxing country home which was built in formal colonial style in 1756 and remodeled in 1938. Several porches and fireplaces have been added during the years. The inn has 2 parlors with fireplaces, a dining room, and a total of 10 guest rooms. Dinners are served to both the guests and the public from a simple menu that changes every four months but might include four standard dishes such as a fish of the day, scallops with pignola nuts, veal Viennese, and New York sirloin. In addition, the chef prepares a special entree each evening. Prices for a complete dinner average $9.75 to $13.50, depending on specific choices from the a la carte menu. *Room Rates*: Double room, $26 to $32. Reservations are required. No pets permitted. *Driving Instructions*: From the south, take I-95 to exit 70, left off ramp, then right at stoplight. From the north, exit 70 off I-95, left off ramp. The inn is the third building on the left.

OLD LYME INN

85 Lyme Street, Old Lyme, CT 06371. 203-434-2600. *Innkeepers*: Kenneth and Diana Milne. Open all year.

The Old Lyme Inn was built as a private mansion in 1850 and restored by the Milnes to its original style, with French Empire furnishings; it is included in the National Registry of Historic Buildings. The inn has five guest rooms, each with private bath, all decorated in the same French Empire style. The parlor, with its marble fireplace and sofa, can be used for dining by small private parties. There is also a cocktail lounge which features a 16-foot Victorian bar. A mid-nineteenth-century atmosphere prevails in the blue and gold dining rooms, providing a perfect setting to enjoy fine provincial French cooking. The menu takes advantage of fresh seasonal foods and the meals are all cooked to order; even the French pastries are baked on the premises. An extensive collection of French wines compliments the menu. For guests there are many nearby attractions such as the *Goodspeed Opera House*, the *Gillette Castle*, and *Mystic Seaport and Aquarium*. The Connecticut River and the Long Island Sound provide good boating and swimming. In summer, guests are given passes to the town beach. *Room Rates:* Single rooms, $27; double rooms, $30. Reservations are required. Pets are permitted. *Driving Instructions:* Take the Connecticut Turnpike (I-95) to exit 70. The inn is within view of the turnpike.

Massachusetts

MASSACHUSETTS IS no stranger to exploration. Probably visited by Norsemen in the year 1000, it was certainly visited by John Cabot in 1497 and 1498. He and all early navigators were drawn to this area because of the abundance of cod off its shores. This gave the ships a welcome chance to refill their stores before continuing their way along the coastline. So grateful for the cod was Bartholomew Gosnold, the coastal explorer, that he named the now famous Cape for it. The first settlers here were, of course, the Pilgrims who were compelled to leave their homes in England to seek religious freedom. After landing in Provincetown in 1620, they wrote the Mayflower Compact, a model for part of the Constitution when it was written many years later.

Although the early years of the Massachusetts Bay Colony were characterized by peaceful relationships with the mother land, the strain developed soon and reached a pinnacle by the early 1760s when a series of repressive trade and taxation acts inflamed residents of the colony. In 1770 British soldiers fired on a crowd of angry citizens, further inflaming the Massachusetts residents. The Tea Act of 1773 which followed the earlier Stamp and Sugar Acts was virtually the last straw. Just two years later, the "shot heard round the world" was fired at Lexington and Concord and the American Revolution had begun. In 1780, the constitution of the Commonwealth of Massachusetts was drawn up and ratified. It is the oldest constitution still in use today. The name Massachusetts, incidently, was taken from the Algonquin tribe living to the south of Boston.

Massachusetts is divided into several sections, each of which has a special appeal to tourists. In the western part of the state are the Berkshires with their summer music festivals and winter sports centers. The central part ranges from Amherst, with its colleges, to Worcester, the state's second largest city. The eastern portion is dominated by Boston and its suburbs but remains remarkably rural within a short drive of the Hub, as Boston is known locally. Cape Cod, although small in size, is probably the best-known vacation spot in the East.

To help you plan your vacation, we recommend that you contact the Massachusetts Department of Commerce and Development, 100 Cambridge Street, Boston, MA 02202. Their telephone is 617-727-3205. They will be glad to send you their vacation planner. Chambers of commerce in particular areas can also be helpful.

WESTERN

The Berkshires (including Lee, Lenox,
New Marlboro, South Egremont, Stockbridge,
and environs)

The Berkshires make up a mountain and lake region of extraordinary beauty and variety. The Maine-to-Georgia *Appalachian Trail* runs the length of Berkshire County with miles of hiking and cross-country skiing trails.

In the mid-nineteenth century, gentlemen from New York and Boston began buying up Berkshire farms, and by the 1880s, nearly 100 fabulous mansions had been built in and around Lenox, "the inland Newport." The quiet, rural places attracted many artistic women and men throughout the years. Nathaniel Hawthorne and Edith Wharton came to Lenox and Mark Twain and Herman Melville came to the surrounding area. Norman Rockwell lives and paints in Stockbridge. His work can be seen at the *Old Corner House. Tanglewood*, where Hawthorne wrote, is the summer home of the *Boston Symphony Orchestra* and the *Berkshire Music Festival*. Ted Shawn's *Jacob's Pillow*, the foremost dance festival in the world, is located in Lee. *Hancock Shaker Village*, a restored Shaker settlement dating from 1790, lies north of Stockbridge, just west of Pittsfield. The area abounds with wildlife sanctuaries, theaters, playhouses, museums, and historic houses.

In the fall, the Berkshires are ablaze with autumn foliage. Soon to follow is the snow and its accompanying skiers. There are several ski areas, all within an easy drive from the villages with their country inns and farmhouses. Most of the big areas have snow-

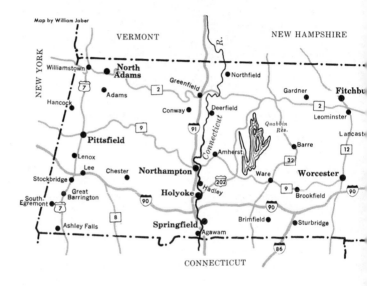

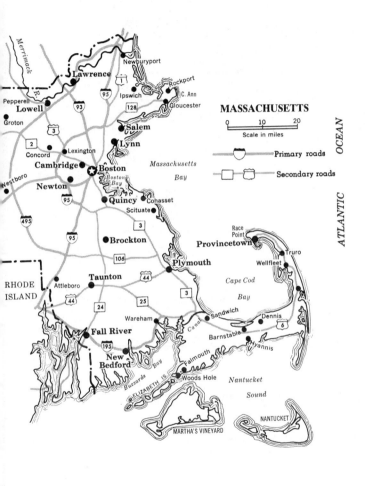

MASSACHUSETTS

Scale in miles

0   10   20

Primary roads

Secondary roads

Merrimack R.

Newburyport

Lawrence

Pepperell

Lowell

Groton

Ipswich

Rockport

C. Ann

Gloucester

Salem

Concord

Lexington

Lynn

Cambridge

Boston

Massachusetts Bay

Boston Bay

Newton

Quincy

Cohasset

Scituate

Westboro

Brockton

Provincetown

Race Point

Truro

Wellfleet

Plymouth

Taunton

Attleboro

Cape Cod Bay

RHODE ISLAND

Wareham

Sandwich

Dennis

Barnstable

Hyannis

Canal

Fall River

New Bedford

Falmouth

Woods Hole

ELIZABETH IS.

Buzzards Bay

Nantucket Sound

NANTUCKET

MARTHA'S VINEYARD

ATLANTIC OCEAN

making facilities in case snow is later than usual in arriving there.

For nonskiers, there are plenty of hills and lakes for sledding, skating, and ice fishing. Weekends in winter are great for sports participants and spectators alike. The Berkshire Vacation Bureau has brought together many different winter events staged annually by the resorts and organizations in the area into one enormous *Berkshire Winter Carnival*, during the month of January and early February, with most events held on weekends.

For antiquers and sightseers, there are many antique shows, fairs, and festivals throughout the summer and fall. One of the biggest is the *Berkshire Craft Fair* held in Great Barrington in August. A wide selection of antique and craft shops can be found in the Berkshire villages and on the winding back roads.

Deerfield Village, Massachusetts

Deerfield is a designated National Historical Site. Settled 300 years ago, it was for a while the last outpost of New England's frontier. The settlement was twice devastated by Indian raids, once by the Bloody Brook Massacre in 1675 and again in the French and Indian War in the Deerfield Massacre, 1704, the most successful raid ever made by Indians on an American frontier village. The town was resettled and became an agricultural center in western Massachusetts. The past was not forgotten, and in 1952 Mr. and Mrs. Henry N. Flynt founded *Historic Deerfield* on mile-long Old Deerfield Street. Historic Deerfield maintains 11 old houses, a research library, and an active education program studying the arts in early America, the culture of the Connecticut Valley, and Historic Deerfield itself. The town is the home of the Eaglebrook School, the Bement School, and the Deerfield Academy, a boys' preparatory school built around the village green and founded in 1797.

DEERFIELD INN, INC.

Main Street, Deerfield, MA 01342. 413-774-3147. *Innkeeper*: Charles A. Kaminski. Open all year, except for three days at Christmas.

Deerfield Inn, built in 1884, is located mid-point on historic Old

Deerfield Street. Many of the houses and buildings on this street are owned and maintained as museums by Historic Deerfield, Inc. The inn with its two-story white-columned porch is shaded by big trees. It is decorated with antiques and portraits of stern ancestors peering down from the walls. The 12 guest rooms each have private baths, starched white curtains, and flowered wallpaper. The dining room, with its brass candlesticks on polished mahogany tables, serves three meals daily to guests and public alike. *Room Rates*: Single rooms, $28; double rooms, $28 to $30. Reservations are required. No pets permitted. *Driving Instructions*: North on I-91, to exit 25; then go north on Route 5 and 10 (same road) to Deerfield.

Greenfield, Massachusetts

Greenfield is a neighbor of Old Deerfield. Several rivers join the big meandering Connecticut near Greenfield. It is an area of rivers, mountains, and many state parks and forests. In the summer there are concerts at *Shattuck Park*. The *Mount Mohawk Ski Area* has, in addition to alpine skiing, indoor ice skating.

RITE VIEW FARM

493 Leyden Road, Greenfield, MA 01301. 413-773-8884. *Innkeeper*: Mrs. Ida Wright. Open all year.

Rite View is a real working dairy farm where the milk is pumped fresh from the cow to the bulk tank. The nineteenth-century farmhouse is situated on 230 acres of rolling fields, pine groves, and woodlands, all ideal for some peaceful hikes. Guests enjoy Mrs. Wright's up-country fare served family style in the old farm dining room. Three bright guest rooms overlook the fields of corn and hay in summer and the snowy vistas in winter. Most summer and winter activities are available within an easy 5–10 mile drive from the farm. *Room Rates*: Including two meals served family style, for adults, $17 per day or $110 per week; for children $12 per day or $75 per week. No pets permitted. *Driving Instructions*: Three miles north of Greenfield. Take Main Street to Conway Street to Leyden Road.

Lee, Massachusetts (see the Berkshires)

MORGAN HOUSE

33 Main Street, Lee, MA 01238. 413-243-0181. *Innkeeper*: Tony Ferrell. Open all year.

The Morgan House, built in 1817 as a private residence, was converted to a stagecoach inn in 1853. Early guests included Buffalo Bill, Robert E. Lee, and President Ulysses S. Grant. In 1974, Mrs. Nat King Cole bought the Morgan House and restored it to its original charm. The inn has seven guest rooms, each furnished with Victorian beds, quilts, and rockers, and decorated with flowered wallpaper. The dining room features up-country fare such as Yankee pot roast and Irish lamb stew. Meals are served family style. A glassed-in sun porch off the bar is open year-round.

Nearby Tanglewood, ski areas, antique shops, and many theaters make this centrally located inn a convenient stop. *Room Rates*: Double rooms, $25 July through October; $15 to $20 in the off season. Reservations are requested. No pets permitted. *Driving Instructions*: Massachusetts Turnpike exit 2 (Lee), then Route 20 to Lee.

Lenox, Massachusetts (see the Berkshires)

GARDEN GABLES INN

141 Main Street, Lenox, MA 01240. 413-637-0193. *Innkeeper*: Mrs. Marie R. Veselik. Open all year.

This 190-year-old gabled inn was originally a private estate. Its last owner, Kate Carey, moved the house away from the road, added on, and built a 72-foot swimming pool at the rear.

Although the inn is on Main Street, it has a protected feeling because it is set back from the road. Mrs. Veselik is a great lover of animals, and many come out of the local woods to visit her property. The older parts of the inn have some colonial antiques while the newer extension is filled with turn-of-the-century furniture. Most rooms have private baths, but there are some where you will have to share a bath (five persons share two baths). The living room has a fireplace and a supply of magazines and books. The inn limits its guest list to 20 persons, which enhances the intimate feeling here. The only meal served is breakfast, for houseguests only. *Room Rates*: During July and August, rooms are rented weekly with rates ranging from $75 to $107 per person, double occupancy. From September to June, the rooms are rented on a daily basis ranging from $9 to $12 per person, double occupancy. Single rooms are available all year at slightly higher rates. Breakfast is not included. No pets permitted. Faces St. Ann's Church.

THE VILLAGE INN

16 Church Street, Lenox, MA 01240. 413-637-0020. *Innkeepers*: Richard and Marie Judd. Open all year.

The Village Inn is located in the center of historic Lenox, one mile from Tanglewood. Built in 1776, the inn has 26 guest rooms all decorated in true colonial fashion, with antique furnishings and even wallpaper of that period. During the winter open fireplaces add a glow to the lounges and dining room. The inn serves three meals daily and one is likely to find such American staples as Yankee pot roast and hot apple pie on the menu. Both the dining room and the pub below it are open to the public. The pub, Poor Richard's Tavern, captures the flavor of Ben Franklin's time with its hand-hewn bar and big working fireplace. *Room Rates*: November to June, $17 to $24; July and August, $29 to $42; September and October, $25 to $30. Reservations are strongly recommended in summer, fall, and for holidays. No pets permitted. *Driving Instructions*: From New York, take Taconic Parkway north to Mass. 23, east to U.S. 7, north to Lenox. From Boston, take Massachusetts Turnpike to exit 2 and U.S. 20 to Lenox.

WHEATLEIGH

West Hawthorne, Box 824, Lenox, MA 01240. 413-637-0610. *Innkeepers*: A. David Weisgal and Florence Brooks-Dunay. Open all year.

In the heart of the Berkshires, bordering a lake, amid lawns and gardens, stands Wheatleigh, a sprawling Italian palazzo. Patios, porticoes, and terraces surround the chateau, which is situated on a 22-acre estate. The centerpiece is Wheatleigh, built in 1893 by industrialist H. H. Cook as a wedding present for his daughter who married Count de Heredia. The multi-millionaire New Yorker is reputed to have paid $1 million for the mansion. About 150 Italian artisans were said to have been imported to carve the mantles, ceilings, and walls. Wheatleigh combines the beauty of a European hotel with the comfort and elegance of an Edwardian-American home. The public rooms at Wheatleigh include a Great Hall with original Tiffany windows and a winding staircase as well as a library with a new bar. These rooms have carved fireplaces, as do many of the guest rooms. Some guest rooms have balconies with views of the lake and grounds; they are furnished with antique sofas and canopied beds, and have marble bathrooms. Breakfast is served to guests only but the inn's dining room is open to the public for lunch and dinner.

Music, theater, art, dance, sports, and antique shops all abound in the surrounding area. The Tanglewood Music Festival is within walking distance from the inn. Swimming and tennis are available on the grounds. *Room Rates*: Rates depend on the season of the year, day of the week, and selection of the room. They range from $15 to $40 per person, breakfast included. Reservations are required. No pets permitted. *Driving Instructions*: From Lenox (at center of Lenox–Curtis Hotel corner), turn left on Stockbridge Road to bottom of hill, then right and continue 1½ miles, keeping left to the Wheatleigh entrance. From Stockbridge, at Red Lion Inn on Route 7 go straight up Prospect Hill Road bearing left past the Stockbridge Bowl and Music Inn up the hill to Wheatleigh entrance on right (about five miles).

New Marlboro (see the Berkshires)

THE FLYING CLOUD INN

South Sandisfield Road, New Marlboro, MA 01230. 413-229-2113. *Innkeepers*: Martin and Beverly Langeveld. Open from early May through October and from mid-December through mid-March.

The Flying Cloud is one of the most widely publicized inns in the United States, having received rave reviews in many magazines and guidebooks. Despite all of its well-deserved acclaim the inn remains a secluded colonial retreat in the heart of the Berkshires. All the rooms are furnished with antiques. One room features a 1790 fourposter bed with an antique log-cabin quilt. The main portion of the farmhouse was built by shipwrights in 1771 and sits in the middle of 200 acres of meadow lands.

The dining room features fresh vegetables from the organic garden and hot breads direct from the oven. Dinners are served family style and only to inn guests (and their guests).

In the summer there are two tennis courts—one very fine clay—and swimming in the spring-fed pond. In winter plenty of cross-country skiing, skating, and snowshoeing is available. Nearby, one can hike the Appalachian Trail in any season. *Room Rates*: Including two meals, gratuities, tennis in summer and cross-country skiing in winter—$34 to $40 per person, Friday to Sunday; $31 to $36 per person, Monday to Thursday. Reservations are required. Pets permitted by special arrangement only. *Driving Instructions*: From New York, Route 44 east to Canaan, Connecticut, left on Route 7 (north) ¾ mile to right at Shell station. Follow signs 12.5 miles to inn; from Boston, Massachusetts Turnpike to exit 2 (Lee) then 102 to 7 south to 23 east to 57. Follow signs.

Princeton, Massachusetts

At the turn of the century Princeton was a resort town in the Wachusett Mountains. The old inns are almost all gone now, but the lovely common and handsome old summer homes still remain. From the summit of Mount Wachusett (altitude 2006) there is a spectacular view of the surrounding countryside. The *Wachusett State Park* offers horse trails, picnic sites, hiking, skiing, and recreational vehicle trails. *Mount Wachusett Ski Area* is off Route 2 and 140. The Massachusetts Audubon Society maintains the *Wachusett Meadows Wildlife Sanctuary*.

THE INN AT PRINCETON

Mountain Road, Princeton, MA 01541. 617-464-2030. *Innkeepers*: Suzanne Reed and Elizabeth Sjogren. Open all year, except between January 15 and March 1.

Built in the early 1890s, the 23-room Inn at Princeton was originally the country summer home of Charles Washburne, founder of American Steel and Wire. The old mansion is situated on 12 acres of mountainous woodlands with a commanding view of the Boston skyline. The spacious bedrooms share this view. One enters the inn through an enormous front door, nearly five feet wide and eight feet high. Off the vast hallway is a living room with a fireplace and two dining rooms. The entire place has been painstakingly restored by Reed and Sjogren and furnished with a blend of turn-of-the-century antiques and modern decor.

The Inn at Princeton is known for its country-classical cuisine and features such specialties as quail sauté, duckling à la Montmorency, scallops Provençale, and several rich desserts. *Room Rates*: $25 to $45 including continental breakfast. Reservations are required. No children or pets permitted. *Driving Instructions*: Follow Mountain Road from junction of Routes 31 and 62 at the center of Princeton.

Sheffield, Massachusetts

In 1724, a group of Mohican Indians sold a tract of their land for 3 barrels of cider, 30 quarts of rum, and $460. The new owners divided the land into two townships; Sheffield was part of the lower Housatonic township. The first white settler, Matthew Noble, arrived alone in 1725 and the first settlement in the Berkshires was on its way. Today Sheffield is one of the leading agricultural communities in Berkshire County. The town has many interesting old homes; the *Colonel John Ashley House*, built in 1735, is the oldest house in the county and a fine example of eighteenth-century architecture. Adjacent to the Ashley House is *Bartholomew's Cobble*, a National Landmark—a natural rock garden overlooking the Housatonic River. There is also a covered bridge over the river.

IVANHOE COUNTRY HOUSE

Route 41, Sheffield, MA 01257. 413-229-2143. *Innkeepers*: Mr. and Mrs. Richard Maghery. Open all year.

The Ivanhoe Country House was built in 1800 on the Appalachian Trail at the foot of a mountain. The inn is quiet and comfortable, with many antique funishings. There are five guest rooms, one with a working fireplace and one with a complete kitchenette. A continental breakfast with cocoa and homemade blueberry muffins

is provided. For other meals, the Magherys recommend several nearby restaurants and inns, including Stagecoach Hill in Sheffield and Undermountain Inn and White Hart Inn in Salisbury, Connecticut, across the state line. There are 25 acres of grounds at Ivanhoe for all kinds of outdoor activities, including sledding in winter. The surrounding area offers an enormous assortment of activities year-round for all interests from antiquing and sightseeing to skiing and canoeing. *Room Rates*: Single rooms, $12 to $18; double rooms, $14 to $22; room with kitchenette, $26. Reservations suggested. Pets permitted. *Driving Instructions*: Turnpike to Lee exit. South on Routes 7 and 41. From New York, Taconic Parkway, east 20 miles on Route 23, south 3½ miles on Route 41.

STAGECOACH HILL INN

Route 41, Sheffield, MA 01257. 413-229-8585. *Innkeepers:* Francis Burns and Wilbur Wheeler. Open all except Wednesday evenings and the month of March.

The Stagecoach Hill Inn is a gracious brick building constructed in the early 1800s as a stagecoach stop. Part of the building served as the town poorhouse 100 years ago. The inn is a bit cozier now, with an atmosphere that will transport you back to merrie England. Steak and kidney pie, blackbird pie, and an "Alderman's Carpetbag" (sirloin stuffed with oysters) are just a few of the many offerings served in this English pub with its Scotch flair. Two working fireplaces complete the picture. In the summer, Tanglewood and Jacob's Pillow are an easy drive from the inn. *Room Rates*: $23 to $26; $31 for a suite with a fireplace. Reservations are requested. No pets permitted. *Driving Instructions*: Massachusetts Turnpike to Lee exit, Route 7 to Great Barrington, then Route 41 south 10 miles.

South Egremont (see the Berkshires)

THE EGREMONT INN

Sheffield Road, South Egremont, MA 01258. 413-528-2111. *Innkeepers*: Susanne and Bernard Eismann. Open all year.

The Egremont is another old stagecoach inn. It retains the feeling of the colonial days (1780) when it was built but has been carefully redone to incorporate certain twentieth-century conveniences such as private baths for each of its 25 guest rooms. However, other modern conveniences like television or telephones in the rooms have been purposefully omitted. Although there is central air conditioning, this is unobtrusive. The bedrooms are old-fashioned in appearance and very comfortable. The public rooms have fireplaces and the broad porch contains rockers as well as tables for eating in warm weather. There are two all-weather tennis courts and a swimming pool on the premises. A ski touring center at the inn has gently rolling wooded trails as well as certified instruction; equipment rental is available. The inn serves three meals daily to guests and the public. *Room Rates*: The inn offers a variety of rates, all of which exclude meals and are dependent upon time of the year and day of the week. These range from $25 to $45 for double rooms, with other options available. No pets permitted, but kennels are nearby. *Driving Instructions*: Take Route 23 directly to the inn in the center of South Egremont.

Stockbridge and West Stockbridge, Massachusetts (see the Berkshires)

MUSIC INN

West Hawthorne Street, Stockbridge, MA 01240. 413-637-2970. *Innkeeper*: Peter Provenzano. Open May through October (with some year-round rooms available on a monthly basis only).
The rustic Music Inn is situated on 180 acres of rolling fields and forests overlooking the Berkshires' Lake Mahkeenac, a short walk from Tanglewood. The inn is housed in the former farm buildings of the Wheatleigh estate, a magnificent gentleman's farm in the late nineteenth century. Very youth-oriented, the inn features a rock-and-roll club called the Great Riot Alley Memorial. The carriage house has a dining room and the Toad Hall Moviehouse showing classic and contemporary film revivals. There is a natural amphitheater where rock, jazz, and country concerts are held during summer months.

Guests stay in rooms in the converted and restored ice house, carriage house, and barn. Music and laughter from the nightclub tend to keep ringing out through the night up till the wee hours. *Room Rates*: Single rooms with private bath, $115 per month or $35 per week; $5 less without bath. Rooms are $15 per day, but the inn prefers weekly stays. No pets permitted. *Driving Instructions*: Massachusetts Turnpike, exit 2. Route 20 west to Route 183 south. First left past Tanglewood, then ½ mile on left.

THE RED LION INN

Main Street, Route 102, Stockbridge, MA 01262. 413-298-5545. *Innkeeper*: Betsey M. Holtzinger; owned and operated by Senator and Mrs. John H. Fitzpatrick. Open year round.

The Red Lion Inn is the grande dame of old colonial inns. First built in 1773 as a small tavern and stagecoach stop for vehicles serving the Albany, Hartford, and Boston runs, the inn was greatly enlarged in 1862. Although the Red Lion has had several owners, it was owned from the time of the Civil War until the early 1960s by members of the Treadway family. Over the years, various modernizations have occurred but without disturbing the charm of this long-time famous resident of the Berkshires.

The inn has an extensive collection of antiques, which grace the public rooms and greatly add to the feeling of the past. The tavern is paneled in old wood with the warm patina of age. There is a feeling of grandeur in both the dining room and the parlors with their Oriental rugs and grand pianos. In its long history, the inn

has been host to five United States presidents. It is easy for a visitor today to see why.

All meals at the Red Lion are open to the public. Breakfasts cost from $3 to $5.50 and luncheons may be simple sandwich affairs for under $5, or more formal meals featuring meat, poultry, or fish and ranging in price from $3.50 to $6 with salad. Dinner at the Red Lion gives the patron the opportunity to choose from 21 entrees including specialties such as entrecote with herb butter, veal a la Oscar, stuffed pork chop, baked or boiled lobster, or scallops in mushroom and wine sauce. There is, in addition, a modest list of appetizers and a good selection of desserts. A complete dinner might range anywhere from $10 to $17. There is a special house Châteaubriand served with sauce charon and a garnish of fresh vegetables priced at $30 for two. *Room Rates*: Rates are seasonal and vary for double rooms from $20 to $48. Pets are permitted. *Driving Instructions*: Massachusetts Turnpike, exit 2 to Lee. Follow Route 102 to Stockbridge.

WILLIAMSVILLE INN

Route 41, West Stockbridge, MA 01266. 413-274-6580. *Innkeepers*: Lenora and Stuart Bowen. Open all year, except in early November.

The Williamsville Inn is near the base of a 2000-foot mountain. Christopher French built the old farmhouse in the late 1700s. He had lived 100 yards away on the Williams River but the neighboring Indians were so noisy he was forced to move his family up the hill. Later Mr. French deeded all but the front room, a room over it, and the cellar beneath, to his son. He retained possession of his section of the house until his death. The Christopher French Room is now a favorite guest room.

Today the inn is a quiet home on 10 landscaped acres with a swimming pool, tennis courts, and a trout pond. The spacious rooms are furnished with many antiques. There are eight working fireplaces—two in guest rooms. The candlelit dining room has a big fieldstone fireplace, adding a special glow on cool nights.

The Williamsville is well known for its French country cuisine prepared by Lenora Bowen. An article by Andy Merton and Gail Kelley in *Boston Magazine* (October 1977) described her as "a

41

marvelous French chef . . . her veal dishes are especially recommended . . . flavors delicate and delightful. In fact, we judged the food here the best on our trip, just topping Le Jardin, Stafford's-in-the-Field and the Arlington Inn, all of which are worth a trip for the food alone." *Room Rates*: Double rooms, $45 in July, August, and October; $33 in May, June, and September; $30 November through April; $5 additional for rooms with fireplaces; all rooms $5 less on weekdays. Reservations recommended. No pets permitted. *Driving Instructions*: The inn is four miles south of West Stockbridge. Take Massachusetts Turnpike, exit 1, turn left on Route 41.

EASTERN

Andover, Massachusetts

Andover is a town filled with tree-shaded streets and lanes with expansive white colonial homes, little shops, and the 450-acre campus of Phillips Andover Academy. Andover was established in 1646 when settlers purchased the land from the local Indians for $30 and a coat. The Phillips Academy, founded in 1778, has many historic buildings on its campus; the *Robert S. Peabody Foundation for Archaeology* contains New England archaeological exhibits; the *Addison Gallery of American Art* traces American history with paintings, sculpture, and decorative crafts from colonial times to the present. The town also has many other historic sites.

The area abounds in craft and antique shops; the North Andover Center has many antique and thrift shops in one place. Hiking, picnicking, bird watching, or just relaxing and star gazing are offered in the surrounding parks and forests. The *Harold Parker State Forest*, *Ward Reservation*, and the peaceful *Cochran Bird Sanctuary* are all in Andover. For winter sports, the Boston Hills Ski Area is four miles away.

THE ANDOVER INN

Chapel Avenue, Andover, MA 01810. 617-475-5903. *Innkeeper*: Henry Broekhoff; owners: Mr. Broekhoff and John Oudheusden (chef). Open all year, except Christmas day.

The Andover Inn is located on the campus of Phillips Academy with its ivy-covered buildings. Built in 1927, the white-columned brick structure contains 33 guest rooms. The recently redecorated inn blends warm woods and comfortable furnishings with modern conveniences. The many fireplaces in the public rooms add a warm glow to the inn's colonial atmosphere. There are fireplaces in the two suites also.

The Andover's restaurant is open to the public for all meals. The menu is varied, with seafood, beef, and a continental selection of veal and game dishes. The special day is Sunday when Chef Oudheusden features a rijsttafel, an Indonesian feast combining rice (masi) with a large number of side dishes such as roast pork with peanut sauce, fruit in hot sauce, beef, shrimp, and fish in various sauces, and much more—an exciting meal. *Room Rates*: $25 to $34 with private bath; $19 to $25 with shared bath; suites are $35 single, $45 double. Reservations are requested. Small trained pets are permitted. *Driving Instructions*: North from Boston, Route 93N to Route 125E to Route 28N; the inn is approximately three miles on right on Route 28. South from N.H., Route 495S to Route 28S, inn is two miles on left.

Rockport, Massachusetts

First settled in 1640, Rockport is a harbor town north of Glouces-ter on the Massachusetts coastline. The village has long been a thriving artists' colony, rivaling Provincetown on Cape Cod. There is a very active, tourist-oriented shopping area which is a collection of historic fishing shacks and more substantial buildings located on a tiny spit of land and breakwater known as Bearskin Neck. Here the shopper can browse in many craft and art galleries as well as a country store and a number of small restaurants and seafood stores. The famous fishing shack "Motif No. 1," a favorite of painters, was, sadly, washed away by the surf during the cruel winter of 1978. In the village itself is the *Rockport Art Association* with its gallery of graphics, painting, and sculpture all contained in the Old Tavern Building. *The Sandy Bay Historical Society and Museum* has exhibits covering mineralogy, Indian artifacts, quarrying artifacts, and marine life, among others.

OLD FARM INN

291 Granite Street, Rockport, MA. Mailing address: Box 590, Rockport, MA 01966. 617-546-3237. *Innkeepers*: The Balzarini Family. Open all year; the restaurant is open April through mid-November.

The Old Farm Inn is situated between Halibut Point and Folly Cove on the northernmost tip of Cape Ann. The date of the farmhouse is estimated to be 1799, but a house has been on the site since 1705. In the early 1900s, Antone Balzarini, an immigrant from Italy, rented the farm and raised dairy cows and 12 children there. The family later moved down the road. In 1964, one of Antone's sons, John, and his family, bought the old place. The Balzarinis restored the farmhouse and furnished it with antiques, including the much-used big black iron stove. They added on a dining room overlooking a meadow where ponies graze and an outdoor terrace, and converted the old barn into guest rooms. The dining room has beamed ceilings, open hearths, and floor-to-ceiling windows. The Old Farm Inn specializes in fresh locally caught seafood. For dessert there is Indian pudding baked in the iron stove and Uncle Charlie's rum bread pudding. Rockport is a dry town so bring your own spirits and the restaurant will provide setups.

Guests can enjoy the inn's five acres of lawns and meadows with towering trees and abundant flowers or hike along the winding coast road to downtown Rockport, one of New England's most charming seacoast towns. *Room Rates*: July through September, $20; October through June, $16. Reservations are suggested especially in July–September. No pets permitted. *Driving Instructions*: Route 128 to Gloucester, then follow signs to Rockport. Turn left at Railroad Avenue, follow sign to Pigeon Cove (about two miles).

THE RALPH WALDO EMERSON INN

1 Cathedral Avenue, Rockport, MA 01966. 617-546-6321. *Innkeeper*: Gary Wemyss. Open from Memorial Day through mid-October.

The Emerson began life in 1806 as a tavern and was moved about ½ mile in 1840 (when the town went dry) to a location in a "better part of town" to get the carriage trade. In the 1850s Emerson and other notables of the time summered here when it was known as the Pigeon Cove House. In 1870 it was moved to its current location on the ocean. The Wemyss family purchased and renovated it in 1964, renaming it for Ralph Waldo Emerson.

The Emerson is a 35-room traditional nineteenth-century resort-hotel furnished with antiques of the period. Overlooking the ocean are big terraces complete with wicker rockers and potted geraniums. The spacious grounds are perfect for croquet, horseshoes, badminton, or just strolling. There is also a heated saltwater swimming pool and saunas. *Room Rates*: In season, rates start at $47 per day for two persons (modified European Plan) or $27 for two European plan. Before July and after Labor Day, rooms are available at slightly reduced rates, EP only. *Driving Instructions*: Take I-95 to Route 128 to 127 in Gloucester. Route 127 about 1½ miles north of Rockport to sign on Phillips Avenue.

Sudbury, Massachusetts

Sudbury was first settled in 1638 by a group of Englishmen and was primarily an agricultural village for many years. Today, Sudbury is a suburban village about 20 miles west of Boston on the old Boston Post Road, now Route 20. Most famous as the home of Longfellow's Wayside Inn, the village boasts an enjoyable, slightly corny *Wayside Country Store* with an old-fashioned nickelodeon. A short distance away in neighboring Southboro is one of our favorite country stores, the *Willow Brook Farm* with its herd of buffalo and its store filled with old-fashioned and newer products including a meat department that specializes in prime aged beef, buffalo meat, and a variety of game in season. This is an enjoyable stop for people of all ages. Neighboring Framingham is home of the *Garden in the Woods* with its extensive collection of wildflowers. Historic Concord and Lexington are just 10 to 15 miles away.

LONGFELLOW'S WAYSIDE INN

Wayside Inn Road (off Route 20), Sudbury, MA 01776. 617-443-8846. *Innkeeper*: Francis Koppeis; owned by the Wayside Inn Corporation, a nonprofit trust. Open every day except Christmas.

The Wayside Inn is a place of such beauty and history that words do not do it justice. The inn is a designated National Historic Site. To stay here is to stay at a great museum. It is the oldest inn in America. Originally the Red Horse Tavern, the name was changed following the publication of Longfellow's *Tales of a Wayside Inn*, which were based on his knowledge of the Red Horse. This inn was run by eight generations of the Howe family for almost 200 years. It was purchased along with 5000 surrounding acres in the 1920s by Henry Ford, who completely restored it and reproduced a water-powered gristmill which operates today grinding meal for the breads served at the inn. Ford later built a replica of a typical New England chapel nearby and it is currently popular with members of every faith for weddings. In 1928, Ford purchased a one-room schoolhouse which had been the real school of Mary and her

little lamb in the early 1800s. He moved the school from its original site at Sterling, Mass., to its present location near the inn.

Built in stages, starting in 1702, the inn is an extraordinary collection of exposed timber rooms with original paneling and museum-quality antiques. There is, refreshingly, no television or radio. The 10 guest rooms, each different and special, have been modernized to give each a private bath. When you are here, it is hard to remember that the center of Boston is only 25 minutes away. The rural quality is made possible by the tract of surrounding land that Ford purchased to protect the inn. For the day visitor, the common rooms of the inn are open for inspection daily, although there is a very small fee to help support the museum. Shortly before his death, Ford deeded the entire property to the Wayside Inn Corp.

The Wayside Inn restaurant is one of the most popular eating places in this area. Some of the house specialties include roast duckling, stuffed filet of sole with lobster sauce, and deep dish apple pie. *Room Rates*: Single rooms, $17.50; double rooms, $22.50. Pets are not permitted. *Driving Instructions*: Massachusetts Turnpike to Route 495; north to Route 20 east; eight miles to Wayside Inn (one mile after turn at Wayside Country Store). From the east, Rt. 128 north to exit 49; eleven miles west on Route 20.

Swampscott, Massachusetts (including Salem)

Swampscott is a north shore coastal village noted for its fishing and shipbuilding. The Swampscott Dory was developed here. The town has two notable museums—*Atlantic 1* and the *John Humphrey House*. The former is a fire-fighting museum with a collection of antique fire engines. The latter is operated by the Swampscott Historical Society and houses local memorabilia.

It was in neighboring Salem that the days of witchcraft reached their pinnacle. It is less well known that Salem is the third oldest settlement on the continent, dating from 1626. The name Salem, incidentally, comes from the Hebrew *Shalom*, meaning peace.

Nathaniel Hawthorne lived in Salem and made the *House of Seven Gables* one of the area's most noted attractions. A visit here should include a glimpse of the secret staircase of the novel. Also in Salem is the *Peabody Museum* with its collection of items pertaining to maritime history. The *Ropes Mansion* is an early eighteenth-century building with many original furnishings. The *Salem Maritime National Historic Site* is a collection of a number of historic buildings including early customs houses. *Essex Institute* is another collection of six early houses, all dating from 1727–1818. Students of witchcraft will enjoy visits to both the *Witch House* and the *Salem Witch Museum*. Pioneer Village is a replica of the early settlement at Salem. This stop is particularly entertaining for children.

CAP'N JACK'S WATERFRONT INN

253 Humphrey Street, Swampscott, MA 01907. 617-595-9734, 592-1411. *Innkeepers*: Jack and Alison Miller. Open all year.

A real old salty Yankee inn with lots of local flavor, Cap'n Jacks is situated high up on the rocky shore looking out to sea. The inn was built in 1835. It has 24 bright and cheery guest rooms, 14 with private baths and 10 with connecting baths. Most are modern with refrigerators in them, but a few contain old-fashioned canopied fourposter beds. The inn being on the water, guests can stroll the three miles of beaches, watch the fishermen bring in their catches, or cruise on Captain Jack's 70-passenger boat, The Square Peg, compliments of Jack. There are many boat rentals nearby and also fishing party boats for hire in town.

Cap'n Jack's operates a seafood restaurant down the block from

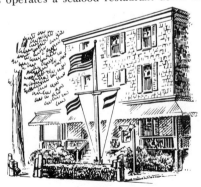

the inn where the house specialties are lobsters and clams. If guests want to dine out there are about 25 restaurants within a 10-mile radius. *Room Rates:* Memorial Day through Labor Day, single rooms, $19 to $27; double rooms, $24 to $34. Off season, single, $10 to $18; double, $12 to $22. *Driving Instructions:* On Route 129 in the center of Swampscott, on the ocean.

Whitinsville, Massachusetts

Whitinsville, located in the Blackstone Valley, is an interesting example of an old mill town with mills and turn of the century mill housing along the Blackstone River. Once the home of the Whitin Machine Works, the leading manufacturer of textile mill machinery, Whitinsville has many large homes and mansions built by wealthy mill owners in the late 1800s. Massachusetts is in the process of constructing a $1 million state park along the Blackstone River in Whitinsville. It is hoped that it will be completed in 1979.

THE VICTORIAN

583 Linwood Avenue, Whitinsville, MA 01588. 617-234-2500. *Innkeeper:* Martha Flint. Open all year.

The Victorian, a mansion on a 50-acre wooded estate, was built in 1871 by a wealthy mill owner. The inn is perfectly preserved. The theft of $2 million of the estate's antiques so discouraged the previous owners—the Whitins—that the place was sold. Two graduate students, with no inn experience but with a lot of ideas on how an

inn and restaurant should be run, purchased the estate. The ideas were apparently excellent—the rooms are lovely and the food delicious. The inn, refurnished in period Victoriana, has seven guest rooms, one with a working fireplace and two with king-sized beds.

The dining room is open to the public for lunch and dinner; breakfast is served only to the inn's guests. The menu features continental cuisine with shrimp, fresh fish, and poultry in a variety of sauces. After meals, one can explore the grounds or, in winter, ice skate on the property. *Room Rates*: $25 to $40. Reservations are suggested. *Driving Instructions*: Take Route 122, south of Worcester, turn west onto Linwood Avenue.

CAPE COD AND THE ISLANDS

The Cape, as it is always called by natives, has long been a vacation favorite on account of its coastal villages and its rural landscape, just a short drive from the heart of Boston. It was discovered in 1602 by the English explorer Bartholomew Gosnold, who first called the Cape "Shoal Hope," but changed its name when his crew caught a particularly impressive load of codfish.

Visitors to the Cape will be treated to a host of attractions in the many towns on this hook-shaped island separated from the mainland by the Cape Cod Canal. There are, in fact, so many attractions, that visitors are urged to read with care the many entries in the three companion books in the Compleat Traveler series. In addition, excellent travel information is available from the Cape Cod Chamber of Commerce, Mid-Cape Highway, Hyannis, MA 02601. Summer visitors who plan to spend any appreciable amount of time on the Cape should investigate the incredibly complete guidebook *The Family Guide to Cape Cod* by Bernice Chesler and Evelyn Kaye (Barre Publishing, Barre, Mass., 1976). This is one of the finest and most comprehensive guides to a geographical region available today and is most helpful to those who wish to see the Cape in detail.

Discussions of special attractions on the Cape are included in the town descriptions preceeding each inn listed here. The following attractions fell outside those town limits but are some of the highlights of any visit to the Cape. As a matter of orientation, the Cape has three main roads running for part or all of its length. These are Route 6 (the Mid-Cape Highway) and Route 6A on the north shore and Route 28 on the south shore. Visitors who prefer a quieter tour of the Cape will be happier following the latter two routes.

For a number of years it appeared that the Cape's frail environment would succumb to the tremendous inroads of tourism. To a degree this has happened and is likely to continue. However, in 1961 the federal government established the *Cape Cod National Seashore* which now controls over 25,000 acres of prime shoreline. In addition to the visitors center mentioned in the section on Eastham, there is the Province Lands Visitors Center in Provincetown where tourists can get maps and descriptive literature.

In Bourne there is the *Aptuxet Trading Post* which is a replica of the first trading post built in 1627 by Plimouth Plantation. Brewster is the home of the *Cape Cod Museum* with its excellent exhibits in the area of natural history. Also there is the *Drummer Boy Museum*, a guided tour of 21 historic life-size paintings of the American Revolution. Brewster is also the home of the *New England Fire History Museum*, which contains a fine collection of antique fire engines. The *Chatham Railroad Museum* is a hit with railroad buffs and the *Old Windmill* in Chatham still is in operation. Falmouth, birthplace of Katherine Lee Bates, who wrote "America the Beautiful," has the *Falmouth Historical Society* museums, which maintain exhibits of paintings and whaling memorabilia. At Woods Hole are three oceanographic institutions which are open to the public at various times. Hyannis, the summer home of President and Mrs. John F. Kennedy, has a memorial to the late president—a 12-foot stone wall bearing the presidential seal and offering a peaceful view of the surrounding harbor. At Mashpee there is the *Wampanoag Indian Museum* and the *Old Indian Meeting House* at the Indian Cemetery.

Sandwich is the home of *Heritage Plantation of Sandwich*, a 76-acre display of Americana housed in replicas of American buildings. In addition to the general exhibits, there is an antique auto museum, a military museum, and a museum of the arts and crafts. The *Sandwich Glass Museum* chronicles the production of the now famous glass factory from 1825 to 1888. An extensive doll museum is housed at the *Yesteryears Museum*, also in Sandwich. South Wellfleet was the site of the first wireless station in America and of the first transatlantic wireless message, sent by Marconi in 1903. The *Wellfleet Bay Wildlife Sanctuary* has several hiking trails. The *Aquarium of Cape Cod* at West Yarmouth has the usual array of trained animals performing in the water to the delight of young and old. Also in Yarmouth are two historic houses open to the public—*Thacher House* and *Winslow-Crocker House*, next door.

Brewster and East Brewster, Massachusetts

Brewster is located on the north coast of Cape Cod on the Cape Cod Bay with its calm, warm waters. (For swimming, it is recommended that one wait until afternoon for the warmer water.) Brewster is noted for its cemeteries, among other things. The *First Parish Church* is the site of the graves of sea captains and early settlers. There are also a great many museums and other historical sites. The *Cape Cod Museum of Natural History* has nature trails, live animals indigenous to the Cape, and many interesting exhibits and lectures. Another wonderful nature trail is the *Wing's Island Trail*, a walk through the marshes to Wing Island—a peninsula on the bay. *Nickerson State Park* has forests, inland fresh water lakes, and trout-stocked ponds. The area offers all manner of outdoor sports available to the public.

INN OF THE GOLDEN OX

Old King's Highway (Route 6A), Brewster, Cape Cod, MA 02631. Mailing Address: 1360 Main Street, RD 1, Brewster, MA 02631. 617-896-3111. *Innkeeper*: Charles Evans. Open all year. The restaurant is closed Mondays in summer and open only on weekends in winter; call to check first.

Overlooking Cape Cod Bay sits the Inn of the Golden Ox. Originally the home of the First Universalist Church of Brewster, the building was constructed in 1828. The inn has four guest rooms sharing two baths. The rooms all have the charm and quiet of an Old World inn, as does the restaurant. All rooms in the Golden Ox are furnished with antiques. The restaurant menu is made up ex-

clusively of gourmet German dishes. A typical meal might begin with either shrimp and dill or marinated lentils as an appetizer followed by *Kassler Rippchen* (smoked loin pork chops), sauerbraten with potato dumpling, and red cabbage in red wine sauce, or a choice of one of six schnitzels (veal cutlet from milk-fed veal). Our favorite is Zigeuner schnitzel (made with piquant paprika, mushrooms, and sour cream). Old family recipes are used for the desserts—*Sacher Torte mit Schlag, Apfelküchen mit Schlag,* and creamy cheese cake. The Golden Ox is a delightful place to enjoy some good food and restful accommodations. *Room Rates*: Memorial Day through Labor Day, $18 plus tax; off season, $15 plus tax. Reservations are requested. No pets. *Driving Instructions:* Mid-Cape Highway (Rt. 6) to exit 9, north to Rt. 6A, right on 6A.

Eastham, Massachusetts

First settled in 1644 by settlers from Plymouth, the area had been previously explored by the French explorer, Samuel de Champlain in 1606. Today, Eastham is a quiet community that has gained recent fame as one of the two major entrances to the *Cape Cod National Seashore*. The Salt Pond Visitors Center provides excellent introductions to the National Seashore as well as maps describing hiking, bicycling, and the special summer interpretive programs conducted by National Seashore rangers. Visitors can swim at two area beaches (parking, $1)—*Nauset Light Beach* and *Coast Guard Beach*. The *Eastham Schoolhouse Museum* is a one-room schoolhouse built in 1869 which now houses a collection of general

Eastham-area memorabilia, early schoolhouse furniture, and other collections of the Eastham Historical Society. The *Grist Mill* is a fully restored mill dating from about 1680. The mill is not actually in operation for safety reasons.

WHALEWALK

Box 169, Bridge Road, Eastham, Cape Cod, MA 02642. 617-255-0617. *Innkeepers*: Jeanne and Mac Cambell. Open all year.

Whalewalk, named for the widow's walk or "whalewalk" atop the inn, is an old Cape Cod farm. Built 150 years ago for a sea captain, Whalewalk is a classic example of Georgian architecture. Situated on four acres of fields and meadows, the farmhouse has a terrace where guests can sit and watch the sun set on the salt marsh. The Cambells wish to retain the original charm of the place and have furnished the rooms with antiques. The first-floor guest room has double beds and a fireplace; two of the five upstairs rooms have private baths. There is a library, living room, game room, and terrace for the guests' enjoyment. Several cottages and apartments are on the property and are completely equipped with kitchen, sheets, and blankets. Breakfast, including homemade breads, is served to guests in the sun room. The Cambells will gladly recommend nearby inns and restaurants for other meals.

The bay is just down the road and fresh-water ponds are only a few minutes' drive away. Whalewalk is near Rock Harbor's fleet of charter boats, and is handy to all other kinds of fishing. Cape Cod National Seashore Park Visitors Center, right in Eastham, offers an

interesting program of events. *Room Rates*: In summer, $16 to $30 per day; off season, $14 to $22. The cottages rent by the week in summer and for two and three days in the off season. Reservations for one night are not accepted in-season or on holidays, but if there is a vacancy one is always welcome. No pets permitted, but kennels are nearby. *Driving Instructions*: Somewhat complicated; write or phone the inn.

East Orleans (including Orleans, South Orleans, and environs)

Orleans was settled in 1693 as a part of Eastham and was for years the site of a number of active saltworks. The area has several craft and antique shops and one museum of interest to visitors. The *French Cable Museum*, built in 1890, once housed the transatlantic cable equipment that linked New York City and France. The cables no longer operate, although they once carried the news of the sinking of the *Lusitania* and of Lindberg's landing in Paris. Now the museum provides an interesting lesson in how the old cable worked. The *Cape Cod Antiques Exposition* is held at the Nauset Regional Middle School in Orleans, usually on the first weekend in August. Last year was Orlean's first annual *Bathtub race*. On Nauset Beach the shore and dunes rise to meet orchards and moors. *National Seashore* stretches from Orleans to Provincetown and the *National Audubon Society* maintains a bird sanctuary in East Orleans.

SHIP'S KNEES INN

Beach Road, East Orleans, MA 02643. 617-255-1312. *Innkeepers*: Barbara and Frank Butcher. Open all year.

The Ship's Knees Inn is a restored old sea captain's home overlooking the sea. The inn was built more than 150 years ago and a new section was added in 1970 totally in keeping with the rest of the shingled and shuttered old house. Inside the lantern-lit doorway, the rooms are comfortably appointed with many antiques. The bright guest rooms have beamed ceilings, quilts, and old fourposter beds. Several rooms have an ocean view and one room has a working fireplace. A continental breakfast is included during the summer months. There is a tennis court and swimming pool for guests. *Room Rates*: June 15 through Labor Day, $30 to $38 with private bath; $14 to $30 sharing bath. Off season, $20 to $25 with private bath; $14 to $16 sharing bath. *Driving Instructions*: Take exit 12 off Route 6; go to first stoplight, turn right, go two stoplights, turn right again. Follow signs to Nauset Beach.

NAUSET HOUSE INN

Box 446, Beach Road, East Orleans, Cape Cod, MA 02643. 61-7-255-2195. *Innkeepers*: Lucille and Jack Swartz. Open from April 1 through November 15.

The Nauset House, built around 1800, is an old Cape Cod farmhouse. This small country inn is furnished with antiques and family memorabilia. On cooler evenings the three fireplaces add their warmth to the homey atmosphere. There is an afternoon cocktail hour in the dining room so that guests can get to know one another. The dining room is reminiscent of an old English pub with a large fireplace and bar where the inn provides setups and ice for the guests (bring your own spirits). Breakfast is the only meal available—hearty country fare served by the open hearth. The inn has 12 guest rooms, 8 with private baths, and 1 with a fireplace. Nauset Beach is within sight of the inn. An early Ameri-

can antique shop is right on the inn's property. *Room Rates*: Rates range from $15 for a single room with shared bath to $30 for an extra-large double with private bath and sitting room. Breakfast is $2 additional. Reservations are suggested at all times. Only children over 11 years of age are welcome. No pets permitted. *Driving Instructions*: Cape Cod's Route 6 to exit 12; turn right and follow signs to Nauset Beach. Inn is located ¼ mile from beach.

Harwich and Harwich Port, Massachusetts

Located on the ocean side of Cape Cod, Harwich and nearby Harwich Port offer visitors much to do. There is fresh and saltwater bathing and fishing as well as shell fishing (permits required; obtainable at the town offices). In the summer there are numerous art exhibitions and band concerts at *Brooks Park* in Harwich. Bike trails are provided in the area. Harwich was the first place on Cape Cod to be included in the National Registry of Historic Districts. The *Harwich Historical Society* is located in and maintains the *Brooks Academy Building* (1844), the site of one of the first navigational schools in this country. The second floor houses scrimshaw, old documents and newspapers, and a fine collection of cranberrying implements (Harwich is a big cranberry area). On the grounds of the academy is the old Revolutionary War *Powder House* (1770).

COUNTRY INN INC.

86 Sisson Road, Harwich Port, Cape Cod, MA 02646. 617-432-2769. *Innkeepers*: Bernice and Bill Flynn. Open all year.

The Country Inn is located near the center of Cape Cod on the ocean side on 6½ acres of farmland. Built in 1773, the main building with its 11 fireplaces was once the farm of the founders of the Jordan Marsh Company in Boston. Through the years several additions have been made to the inn, including three tennis courts and a swimming pool for guests. There are eight guest rooms in the old inn, six with private baths. Dinner is served in the inn's dining room and features fresh local seafood and steaks. The dining room is open to the public for dinner. *Room Rates*: June 15 through Labor Day, single rooms, $16; double rooms, $22. Off season, $2 less per room. Reservations required in July and August and suggested at other times. No children under 12 years of age. No pets permitted. *Driving Instructions*: Take Route 6 to exit 10 (Route 124) to Route 39 (Sisson Road). The inn is about 1 mile from Harwich center.

Martha's Vineyard, Massachusetts

Martha's Vineyard is a triangular island about 19 miles long and less than 10 miles wide. Named after one of his daughters by Bartholomew Gosnold, who also named Cape Cod, the island was once an active whaling center with ports at Edgartown and Vineyard Haven. Local Indians were often members of the crews on the great sailing vessels that left from these ports and even Herman Melville once sailed from the Vineyard.

Of the two old whaling ports, Edgartown is the more interesting architecturally since a fire in 1883 destroyed most of the important buildings in Vineyard Haven. Oak Bluffs is also an interesting village with its array of gingerbread houses. Visitors to the Vineyard are cautioned to avoid bringing cars to the island because the volume of summer traffic here is so intense that movement by car is often discouraging. A better plan is to leave cars on the mainland and bring only bicycles. Those who must bring cars are urged to make auto reservations far in advance to avoid disappointment. Auto reservations on the car ferry from Woods Hole to the Vineyard are difficult to get. Holiday weekends are booked as far in advance as February 1. Nonholiday car reservations are booked three to four weeks in advance. Passengers wishing to make auto reservations may call toll free on one of the following numbers. From Massachusetts, call 800-352-7104. From most other northeastern states and those as far south as Washington, DC, call 80-0-225-3122. If you are in an area not served by these WATS lines then call 617-540-2022. Reservations are not needed for foot passengers on these or the other two ferries serving the Vineyard.

Among the attractions on the island is the *Thomas Cooke House* in Edgartown. The museum has 12 rooms of antique furniture, scrimshaw, and other artifacts. The Liberty Pole Museum in Vineyard Haven is the oldest surviving building there and was originally a church. Housed here is a wide variety of antique material

58

including china, scrimshaw, musical instruments, and early lighting devices. *Seamen's Bethel* was originally a meetinghouse for seamen visiting the ports of the island. It now houses a collection of historical maritime material. The *Hansel and Gretel Doll Museum* in Oak Bluffs has a large collection of nineteenth-century dolls and their costumes.

THE EDGARTOWN INN

North Water Street, Edgartown, Martha's Vineyard, MA 02539. 617-627-4794. *Innkeeper*: Catherine Scapecchi. Open April 1 through November 1.

The Edgartown Inn was originally an old whaling captain's home, built in 1798 for Captain Thomas Worth. A few years later it began a long career as a colonial inn. The Edgartown Inn has played host to many notable guests through the years. Daniel Webster was at first denïed admittance because he was dark skinned and thought to be an Indian. He later returned as a guest as did Nathaniel Hawthorne. Hawthorne came for a rest but stayed on a year to write *Twice Told Tales*. John Kennedy stayed here when he was a Massachusetts senator.

The inn is centrally located in the heart of Edgartown. Minutes away by foot is the white sand beach by the old lighthouse; for real surf bathing, the South Beach is a short ride by car or bike. Nearby are golf courses, tennis, fishing, and summer theater. The inn's front porch overlooks North Water Street with its picket-fenced old captains' houses. The rooms at the inn are much the same as they were in Captain Worth's time, but tiled baths have

been added. Beyond the back patio garden are the "Captain's Quarters," an old barn with guest rooms without private baths for more modest rates. Country breakfasts featuring homemade breads, muffins, and griddle cakes are served in the paneled dining room. The Edgartown will gladly recommend local inns and restaurants for other meals. *Room Rates*: In summer, $28 to $36; off season, $24 to $32. Reservations required in summer. No pets permitted. *Driving Instructions*: To Wood's Hole on Cape Cod and then by ferry to Martha's Vineyard.

Nantucket Island, Massachusetts

The name Nantucket comes from the Indian word "nanticut" meaning faraway land. Thirty miles off the coast of Cape Cod, it's an island paradise far from the rush and neon of today's world. Four miles wide and fourteen miles long, this is a place for long rambling walks and bike rides. Primarily a summer resort, the island is lovely any time of year. From the main town itself to the little villages of Madaket, Polpis, Quidnet, and Wauwinet and the trails through pine groves and over the heathlands, unforgettable scenes unfold at every turn. The beaches are a blinding white. Altar Rock, the highest point at 102 feet, affords a panoramic view of the island's coastline and the rolling moors.

Once one of the greatest whaling ports in the world, the town with its blue-shuttered houses (blue shutters are said to be only for whaling captains and first mates) and winding cobblestone streets flourished in this proud position from 1740 to 1830. With the decline of whaling, families moved away and the island stood practically deserted for many years. The island's relative inaccessibility and the whaling depression during America's big surge of building helped preserve the old buildings and towns. It stands today as the best preserved of all New England areas. The *Whaling Museum* in the "candle house" has a completely rigged whale boat, a whale skeleton, a room full of scrimshaw, and many other whaling artifacts. The *Jethro Coffin House* (1686) is the oldest house on the island and a National Historic Landmark. These and other historic sites and homes are run by the *Nantucket Historical Association* located in Old Town Building.

The island has an unlimited variety of water sports in a wide choice of waters. The south shore provides ocean bathing in the strong surf. The northern side on the harbor, with its still water and sandy shore, is almost completely landlocked, making it ideal for new sailors and children. In late fall, with most visitors gone, the island takes on a different, quiet beauty—the long uninterrupted stretches of beach, the warm golden colors of the moors, and the peaceful streets and roads offer the visitor a restful vacation in a natural setting.

Because of the island's size and lack of parking facilities, tourists are cautioned to leave cars on the mainland if at all possible. There are several bike rental places on the island and good bus service. Those who must bring cars should make reservations far in advance. Foot and bike passengers do not need reservations. The Hyannis Ferry operates in summer only; no cars. On the Woods Hole steamer and car ferry, holiday weekends are booked as far in advance as February. Nonholiday car reservations are booked three to four weeks in advance. Those wishing to make car reservations may call the following phone numbers toll free: In Massachusetts, 800-352-7104. In northeastern states as far south as Washington, DC, 800-225-3122. Out of the toll-free area call 617-540-2022.

FOUR SEASONS GUEST HOUSE

> 2 Chestnut Street, Nantucket, MA 02554. 617-228-1468. *Innkeeper*: Mrs. Herbert Cabral. Open all year.

The Four Seasons Guest House is a pleasant "1850" residence on a quiet street near wharfs, museums, restaurants, and the beach buses. The house is located in the heart of the historic district with its old homes and winding narrow streets. There are nine guest rooms, four with private baths. An efficiency apartment, complete with kitchen, opens onto a grassy backyard. *Room Rates*: Summer seasons and holidays, $20 to $32; off season, $16 to $24. Reservations required in summer. No pets permitted. *Driving Instructions*: Hyannis or Woods Hole ferry to Nantucket. Car is really unnecessary; bring bikes or rent them here.

JARED COFFIN HOUSE

> 29 Broad Street, Nantucket, MA 02554. 617-228-2400. *Innkeepers*: Philip W. and Margaret G. Read. Open all year.

The Jared Coffin House recaptures the spirit and feeling of the days of Nantucket's reign as queen of the world's whaling ports. Built in 1845 by Jared Coffin, one of the island's most successful ship owners, the main house is a classic example of Greek Revival architecture. This house and later additions were restored, in the 1960s, to their original style in both architecture and furnishings. The living room and library are both furnished with Chippendale, Sheraton, and American Federal antiques. Reflecting the world-wide voyaging of the Nantucket whalers, a Chinese coffee table and laquered Japanese cabinet grace the library.

Upstairs in the original house are 10 restored guest rooms furnished with antiques and locally woven fabrics. The 1857 Eben Allen Wing has 16 simply decorated rooms with antiques used wherever possible. The Old House (1700s), located behind the wing, has three bedrooms with canopied beds and examples of crewel embroidery. The Daniel Webster House, across the patio, was built in 1964. It has 12 spacious rooms furnished with a blend of contemporary and colonial reproductions.

Jared Coffin House offers a wide variety of dining for guests and public. In summer, luncheons are served on the canopied patio. The main dining room, its tables set with Spode Lowestoft china and pistol-handled silverware, features New England and continental cuisine. Fresh seafood and veal dishes are the specialties—the Nantucket Bay scallops are excellent. The tap room has an informal atmosphere with old pine walls and hand-hewn beams. Year-round entertainment and hearty grilled foods are featured here.

Holidays at the inn are wonderful. There is a real old-fashioned

New England Thanksgiving. For the Twelve Days of Christmas the inn is decorated with holly, della robia garlands, and—on the front door—a cranberry wreath. At any time of the year the Jared Coffin House is a delightful place to spend a Nantucket vacation. *Room Rates*: Single rooms, $16 to $20; double rooms, $35 to $50. Reservations are required. When making reservations be sure to specify if you prefer a room in the older buildings. *Driving Instructions*: Steamer with car ferry (reservations required) from Woods Hole year-round. Hyannis ferry in summer only. It is a 2½–3 hour ferry trip. See Nantucket for further information.

MARTIN'S GUEST HOUSE

61 Centre Street, Nantucket, MA 02554. 617-228-0678. *Inn-keeper*: Vivian Halliday. Open all year.

Nantucket Island, its homes, and its twisting streets have changed very little from the old whaling days. One seems to step off the ferry or plane and back into the nineteenth century. What better place to savor the atmosphere than in an old Nantucket home? Martin's Guest House fulfills the requirements. Built in 1805 with additions in the nineteenth and early twentieth centuries, the house sits on a hilly brick-sidewalked street. There is a large lawn and pleasant side porch for relaxing. It is an easy walk to the beaches and downtown, with its many shops and restaurants. Martin's has an enormous living room with a working fireplace; 5 of the inn's 14 spacious guest rooms also have fireplaces. No meals are served here but Nantucket has many excellent restaurants and inns

with dining rooms. The place recommended most often for dining is the Jared Coffin House. *Room Rates*: Double rooms with private bath, $38; other rooms are less. Off season rates are lower. Reservations for July and August should be made before June 15 if possible. *Driving Instructions*: Don't bring your car to Nantucket; most likely you won't need it and parking can be very difficult. Take the steamer from Hyannis or Woods Hole.

ROYAL MANOR GUEST HOUSE

31 Centre Street, Box 1061, Nantucket, MA 02554. 617-228-0600. *Innkeeper*: Leon Macy Royal. Open all year.

The Royal Manor is a large old Nantucket home situated on landscaped grounds in the center of town. Built 130 years ago, the house has four big chimneys, seven fireplaces, and several porches (some enclosed). It is furnished with antiques. The spacious guest rooms have inside wooden shutters, Oriental rugs, and modern comfortable beds. There are nine guest rooms, five with private baths. One special room has its own entrance and facilities as well as a small private porch covered with yellow talisman roses in season (mostly June and September).

This is strictly a guest house and food is not served, but owner Leon Macy Royal recommends several nearby restaurants including The Whale and The Mad Hatter, both on Easton Street in town, and the Chanticleer in Siasconset Village seven miles away. *Room Rates*: June 15 to September 15, $10 to $15 per person; $2 less per person in the off season. Reservations are advised. No pets or children under 10 years of age are permitted. *Driving Instructions*: Hyannis or Woods Hole ferry to Nantucket. There is air service to Nantucket also.

Provincetown, Massachusetts

Provincetown has a long history as a summer colony. Before Europeans came to this region, members of the Western Cape Cod Indian tribes would summer at Provincetown to hunt and fish while weather permitted. Many historians feel that the Viking explorer Thorvald, brother of Leif Ericson, was the first European explorer to this area in 1004, predating the visit by Gosnold (mentioned in our section on Cape Cod) by almost 600 years. However, the most famous visit of all was when the first Pilgrims set foot from the *Mayflower* and landed on what is now Commercial Street in Provincetown. It was while the *Mayflower* was in port in Provincetown that the Mayflower Compact was signed. The *Pilgrim Monument* is a 210-foot-high granite structure erected in 1910 and offering those who climb to its summit a view of the entire Cape.

In its early history Provincetown was almost entirely supported by the riches of the sea. During those days, the "Cape-style" house came into prominence in this area and quickly spread to other parts of New England. An excellent example of this style of architecture is the *Oldest House* built in 1746 and open to the public. The *Provincetown Heritage Museum* is housed in a Registered National Landmark building and displays a variety of antiques and artifacts including fire equipment, fishing gear, and the work of American artists. The harbor at Provincetown is still active and is a fine tourist stop in the late afternoon when the catch is being unloaded. The blessing of the fleet occurs annually on the last weekend in June.

Provincetown has gained more recent fame as an artist colony for members of the visual and performing arts. The *Provincetown Art Association* shows the works of its members past and present and includes the work of many of the country's most renowned contemporary artists. The *Provincetown Playhouse* is as active today as it was when Eugene O'Neill was a member of its studio workshop. Contemporary plays and revivals of earlier twentieth-century authors are performed there by a professional company; the *Eugene O'Neill Museum* is next door.

BRADFORD GARDENS INN

178 Bradford Street, Provincetown, MA 02657. 617-487-1616.
Innkeeper: Jim Logan. Open all year.
If you love the sea and a good country inn, you'll love Provincetown and Bradford Gardens. Built in 1820, Bradford Gardens is a relaxed, informal country inn furnished with antiques and artwork. In the old inn are eight rooms, six with working fireplaces, overlooking the garden and, in the winter, the sea. There is the Jenny

Lind Room with early spool furnishings and a fireplace, the Yesteryear Room with its brass bed and brass accents, and the Chimney Nook with garden and water views and a fireplace nook.

The Morning Room has a central fireplace and a bay window overlooking the garden. Here guests mingle and enjoy the inn's country breakfasts, the only meal served. No part of town is more than a mile from the inn so a car is hardly needed. The special parkland bicycle and walking trails are exquisite and, of course, there are miles of beaches for summer swims and winter walks. *Room Rates*: Double rooms, $37 to $60, including breakfasts and firewood; add $5 a day from July 1 through Labor Day. *Driving Instructions*: Follow Route 6 to Provincetown.

WHITE WIND INN

174 Commercial Street, Provincetown, MA 02657. 617-487-1526. *Innkeeper*: Sandra Rich. Open March 1 through November.

The White Wind Inn, a gleaming white Victorian mansion, was once the home of a prosperous shipbuilder. Built in the middle

1800s, the inn is carpeted throughout, has high ceilings, chandeliers, and a blend of antiques and modern conveniences. A complimentary continental breakfast is served in the lounge. There are 11 guest rooms, some with private sundecks. Situated directly across from a quiet stretch of beach, the inn is only a three-minute walk to the center of town with its myriad of activities. *Room Rates*: Memorial Day through Labor Day, $16 to $40; off season, $12 to $26. Reservations are required. *Driving Instructions*: Mid-Cape Highway to Provincetown. Located on corner of Commercial and Winthrop Streets.

West Dennis, Massachusetts

West Dennis is on the south shore of the Cape and is part of the Greater Dennis region including Dennis and East Dennis on the north shore and West Dennis, Dennisport, and South Dennis on the south shore. The area was settled in the late 1630s and named after a pastor of the time from Yarmouth. Three of the area's favorite stops are the *Jerico House and Barn Museum* in West Dennis, housing antique furniture and a fine collection of antique tools and household gadgets; the *Scargo Hill Observation Tower* in Dennis, with its fine view of the Bay; and the *Josiah Dennis Manse*, also in Dennis. *The Cape Playhouse* in Dennis, one of the oldest summer theaters in the country (dating from 1926), presents a full summer season of theater and offers guided tours as well.

LIGHTHOUSE INN

Lighthouse Road, West Dennis, MA 02670. 617-398-2244. *Innkeepers:* Robert and Mary Stone. Open mid-June–mid-Sept.

The historic Bass River Lighthouse, built in 1850, forms the center sections of the Lighthouse Inn, an old-fashioned Cape Cod resort. Many additions have obscured the old lighthouse, but the lobby and dining room are actually inside it. Situated on seven acres of lawns and ocean beach, the inn is surrounded by grey- and white-shingled cottages, all with fireplaces (wood is furnished and set up). The inn's dining room specializes in lobster and other local seafood. *Room Rates:* $30 to $45 per person, MAP; $5 less per person in the off season. *Driving Instructions:* Turn right off Route 28 at the Gulf station in West Dennis.

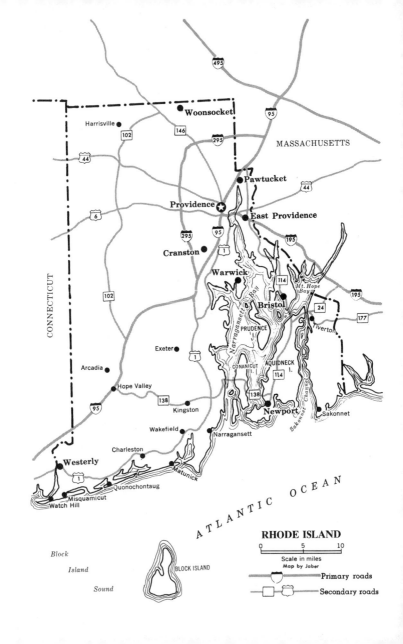

495

Woonsocket
Harrisville ●
102
146
95
295
MASSACHUSETTS
44

Pawtucket
44
Providence ★
East Providence
195
295
95
1
Cranston ●
Warwick
114
Mt. Hope Bay
Bristol
195
177
24
Narragansett Bay
PRUDENCE
Tiverton
Exeter ●
1
CONANICUT
AQUIDNECK I.
114
Arcadia ●
Hope Valley ●
138
Kingston ●
138
Newport
Sakonnet Channel
Sakonnet
95
Wakefield ●
Narragansett
Charleston ●
Westerly ●
Matunick
1
Quonochontaug
Misquamicut
Watch Hill

CONNECTICUT

102

6

ATLANTIC OCEAN

RHODE ISLAND

0   5   10

Scale in miles
Map by Jaber

Primary roads

Secondary roads

Block

Island

Sound

BLOCK ISLAND

Rhode Island

THE NATION's smallest state has the longest official name—State of Rhode Island and Providence Plantations. Rhode Island is 48 miles long and 37 miles wide but, with the huge Narragansett Bay almost cutting the state into unequal sections, the tiny state has 400 miles of coastline. In 1635 Roger Williams was banished from the Puritan colony of Massachusetts Bay. He and his followers founded the first white settlement on the Narragansett Bay. Williams named it Providence Plantations in "commemoration of God's providence." The early settlement was known for its political and religious freedom. In 1638 the country's first Baptist congregation was founded. In Newport one can still see both the *Touro Synagogue* (1763), the oldest American Jewish house of worship, and the country's oldest *Quaker Meeting House* (1699). The first U.S. Catholic mass was held in Newport's *Old Colony House*. Farming and the maritime trades thrived here. Its ports were some of the busiest and largest in the colonies. Feisty Rhode Island led the colonies in proclaiming its independence. At land and sea they were at war with the British long before Lexington and Concord—the most serious incident being the Islander's burning of HMS *Gaspee* in 1772. In 1793 in Pawtucket's *Slater Mill* a factory system was begun that heralded the nation's Industrial Revolution.

Rhode Island has been a vacationer's paradise for hundreds of years. It has fresh and saltwater sports year-round, pine forests and rolling fields, 15 state parks, antique and craft shops, and historic villages and towns.

Before you travel to Rhode Island you should definitely write to the Department of Economic Development, Tourist Division, 1 Weybosset Hill, Providence, RI 02903. The telephone number at the tourist division is 401-277-2601. They will send an excellent packet of information. You should be sure to request three items that are particularly helpful: "This Is Rhode Island," "Guide to

Rhode Island" with its full list of seasonal events of all types as well as sightseeing attractions, and the State Department of Transportation Road Map.

Jamestown, Rhode Island

Jamestown is located on Conanicut Island, famous as the land link between the Jamestown and the Newport bridges. Conanicut Island is devoted to summer recreation, with swimming and fishing facilities available in Jamestown. The 300-year-old ferry no longer operates but can be seen at the *Jamestown Museum*. The *Old Windmill* has been restored by the Jamestown Historical Society and still operates (weather permitting).

At *Beavertail Point* the hurricane of 1938 revealed the base of the third lighthouse established in the United States in 1749. The point and present granite tower offer a spectacular view of Rhode Island's coastline.

BAY VOYAGE INN

Conanicus Avenue, Jamestown, RI 02835. 401-423-0540 and 423-0541. *Innkeepers:* Fred and Nancy Coleman. Open all year. Bay Voyage is situated high on Conanicut Island overlooking the Narragansett Bay and Newport. Named for its nineteenth-century journey across the bay from its birthplace, the 100-year-old inn has quite a history. The Colemans have reprinted the old article that tells of the inn's voyage with the grey-bearded "old sea horse" Captain Sutton.

The inn, "full of antiques," has 23 guest rooms, 12 with private baths. Bright and clean, all are decorated in early Victorian fashion. The dining room and Bay Lounge offer panoramic views of the bay and a menu featuring fresh local seafood. There is a Sunday buffet brunch (10 A.M. to 2 P.M.) offering all you can eat for $3.75, including Rhode Island johnnycakes. *Room Rates*: May 30 through Labor Day, $25 to $45; off season, $18 to $25. Pets are permitted. *Driving Instructions*: Route 138 east over the Jamestown Bridge. Take the last exit before the Newport Bridge to the inn.

Newport, Rhode Island

Rhode Island calls itself "the nation's first vacation land." Evidence to support this claim comes from the visit in 1524 of the Italian navigator, Giovanni da Verrazano. While in the pay of the king of France, he was so enchanted by the beauties of Narragansett Bay that he stayed in the area for a full fortnight, thus earning himself the first vacation with pay in the New World.

The problem with visiting Newport is that the area is so filled with tourist attractions that it is often overwhelming to pick and choose the particular sights of importance to the visitor. Newport operates an excellent Visitors Center with well-trained guides to help with the selection. If the trip is to begin with an exploration of some of the great mansions and houses of Newport, it is helpful to decide in advance how many will be visited so that a group ticket may be purchased, thus gaining the bearer admission to several buildings at reduced rates. Certainly the most popular and spectacular mansions in the area are *The Breakers, The Elms, Marble House, Chateau-Sur-Mer, Kingscote,* and *Rosecliff.* Admission to individual mansions is $2 each but there are reduced-rate package plans available at each house mentioned. Another great mansion is *Belcourt Castle* which is not part of the group plan mentioned above and has an admission charge of $2. In addition to these great monuments to the opulence of days now past there are approximately 20 other historic houses and churches open to the public with admission of, at most, $2.

In addition to the old houses of Newport, there are the *Newport Automobile Museum,* one of the largest collections in New England, and the *International Tennis Hall of Fame.* Several replica ships are open to the public in the Wharf District including the HMS *Rose* and the *Continental Sloop Providence.* The *Touro Synagogue* is the oldest in the United States and a National Historic Site. There is no charge to take the historic *Cliff Walk* along a narrow trail at the top of the cliffs and adjacent to many of the famous Newport mansions. Don't expect to see the mansions well from this vantage point, however, as the hedges and vast lawns prevent close scrutiny of most. The walk is difficult in spots and should be avoided by families with small children and the elderly.

71

CLIFFSIDE GUEST VILLA

2 Seaview Avenue, Newport, RI 02840. 401-847-1811. *Innkeeper*: Mary Healy. Open from April through mid-September. The Victorian Room, a double with private bath, is available year-round.

In 1880, "Villa du Cote" was built by Governor Thomas Swann of Maryland as a summer cottage. Cliffside Villa, overlooking the Atlantic Ocean and Newport's famed Cliff Walk, still retains the character and charm of these earlier times. After a day exploring historic Newport with its famous mansions, antique shops, and museums, or just relaxing on the nearby beach, it is a pleasure to return to Cliffside with its antique-filled rooms and polished wood. The inn does not serve food, but coffee and tea are always available. *Room Rates*: Double rooms, $20 to $30, July through mid-September; $5 less off season. Reservations are required. No children or pets permitted. *Driving Instructions*: Memorial Boulevard to Cliff Avenue (near Cliff Walk). Cliffside is on the corner of Cliff and Sea View Avenues.

Quonochontaug-Westerly and environs

Rhode Island's southernmost coast is dotted with little fishing villages and summer vacation cottages. With miles of beaches and enormous salt ponds the area is a fisherman's paradise. Breachways, ideal for fishing and exploring, are huge rock jetties which cut through the beaches giving boats, fish, and the tide access to the salt ponds. Routes 1 and 1A are excellent sightseeing and antiquing routes, as are the side roads, winding past old stone walls and orchards. In Charlestown on Route 1A is the *Fantastic Umbrella Factory*, a collection of craft and antique shops housed in the barns and sheds of an old working farm complete with animals. Another find is *Windswept Farm*, restored old stone barns where several antique dealers are under one roof. The hurricane of 1938 destroyed most of the summer homes that once lined the beaches here. *Watch Hill*, because of its height, survived and is still one of the loveliest towns in Rhode Island. Rose-covered grey-shingled old summer cottages perch high on the rocky hills overlooking the sea and Block Island beyond. At the end of the winding, roller-coaster road lies the village, a miniature resort town with many shops and a harbor with facilities for guest docking. The *Flying Horse Carousel*, America's oldest merry-go-round, built prior to 1870, still whirls at the edge of town.

There are numerous historical sites in this area of Rhode Island, including many concerning local Indian tribes. The *Indian Church* (1859), and *Royal Indian Burial Ground*, resting place of the Sachems of the Narragansett Tribe, are both located in Charlestown. *Burlingame State Park* with Watchaug Pond offers inland fresh water recreation year-round.

THE SHELTER HARBOR INN

Post Road, Shelter Harbor, Westerly, RI 02891. 401-322-8883. *Innkeeper*: James Dey. Open all year.

Shelter Harbor Inn sits on grassy fields that slope down to the shore of Quonochontaug, one of Rhode Island's biggest salt ponds. The white clapboard farmhouse, overlooking the pond and ocean beyond, is surrounded by old stone wall rimmed fields with their wild roses and clumps of blueberry and June berry bushes. The inn, once an elegant farm, has several comfortable guest rooms in the house and more across the lawn in the converted old barn. There are a few family suites with connecting baths also in the barn. Meals are served in the dining room and the more intimate library. The restaurant is open to the public for dinner. Traditional New England fare is featured, and specialties are finnan haddie and homemade johnnycakes. Guests are invited to join Mr. Dey on trips to nearby farms to pick vegetables for dinner. Motor boats and sunfish (little sailboats) are available for guests, and there is tennis on the property, also. *Room Rates*: Memorial Day through October 15, single rooms, $24; double rooms, $34. Single, $18; double, $24, remainder of year. Breakfast is included. *Driving Instructions*: Route 1, five miles east of Westerly.

Vermont

VERMONT WAS first explored in 1609 by Samuel de Champlain, who voyaged down the lake that was to bear his name. Almost 60 years were to pass before a permanent settlement was made by the French on Isle La Motte in the northern part of Lake Champlain. Later, in 1724, the English established a settlement at Fort Dummer. Soon thereafter, the area destined to become Vermont was engaged in various struggles over its control by the French, settlers from neighboring New Hampshire, and claims by New Yorkers. It was in response to these controversies that some residents of Vermont formed a small soldiering force called the Green Mountain Boys. Formed first to defend New Hampshire's claim to the land against claims of New Yorkers, the band of fierce fighting men were soon to be called into service of a new cause—the Revolution against the Colonial forces of England. After the Revolution, representatives from Vermont met at Windsor and declared themselves to be a separate republic. Vermont remained separate for 14 years, with its own customs and mail service, but was eventually welcomed to the newly formed country in 1791, becoming the fourteenth state.

Although tourism is a leading industry, any visitor is quick to realize that this state, with its great natural resources, is a strong agricultural leader and producer of forest products, not the least of which is its famed maple syrup. Vacation planners will be pleased by the high quality of information that is distributed by the state of Vermont. When the state passed its law prohibiting billboards, it felt a responsibility to disseminate the information previously given by signs, as well as general information of use to tourists. The results are seen in the publications sent to any interested vacationer or handed out at the many state-sponsored information booths. Requests for this literature should be directed to the Vermont Department of Commerce, 61 Elm Street, Montpelier, VT 05602. The telephone number is 802-828-3236.

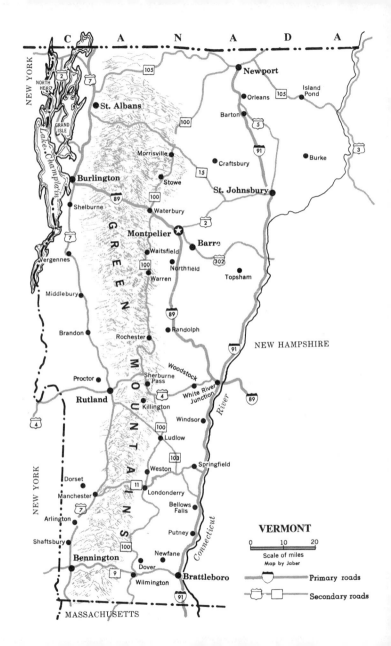

VERMONT

Scale of miles
Map by Jaber

Primary roads

Secondary roads

SOUTHERN

Arlington, Vermont

Arlington is north of Bennington on Route 7. It is an area known for its summer theaters and art galleries, golfing, antique auctions, and crafts shops, as well as for trout fishing and both downhill (25 minutes away at Snow Valley) and cross-country skiing. In the summer hikers enjoy the famed Long Trail and hunters go after the abundant game found in the area. West Arlington has a covered bridge over the Battenkill River. Norman Rockwell, who lived in Arlington for many years, used some of the local scenes on many of his covers for the *Saturday Evening Post*.

ARLINGTON INN

Arlington, VT 05250. 802-375-6532. *Innkeeper*: Stephen C. Lundy. Open all year except from October 15 to Christmas and during April and May. The dining room is closed Mondays and Tuesdays.

The Arlington Inn has been restored and decorated in a sturdy, simple way using period antiques. Its seven very comfortable rooms allow the visitor to feel at home even while on vacation. In addition to the rooms in the inn, a cottage house in the rear has housekeeping facilities. The dining room menu changes daily under the supervision of chef Scott Vineberg and his assistant, George. Typical menus include main dishes like beef Wellington for two, tournedos chasseur, salmon, and veal marsala. *Room Rates*: $21 to $30; special suite, $38. Continental breakfast included. *Driving Instructions*: Take Route 7 north of Bennington about 10 miles to Arlington. The inn is on the right-hand side of the road.

WEST MOUNTAIN INN

Arlington, VT 05250. 802-375-6516. *Innkeepers*: Audrey and Clint Marantz and Wes and Mary Ann Carlson. Open all year.

Clint Marantz and his wife, Audrey, have a dream. They hope in a matter of two years to unite the arts with recreational living

through the creation of an old country inn surrounded by viable, dynamic peforming arts and visual arts centers. Phase one of this ambitious project has been the total renovation of the West Mountain Inn in Arlington.

Set on 150 acres of rolling hills bordered by state forest land and running down to the Battenkill, Vermont's most famous trout-fishing river, the inn was built in 1920 as the summer estate for a Texas couple. The white clapboard building with its seven-gabled slate roof has an intimate dining room with a fireplace and a fabulous view of the surrounding mountains and the Battenkill. The regular meals consist of an eclectic blend of hearty foods including beef Stroganoff and oxtail ragout as well as the standard steaks and fish. However, what sets this inn's cooking apart is its weekly ethnic dinners. On these special occasions the regular menu is tossed aside and the energies of the kitchen are used to create a veritable banquet in the style of a particular region. Recent dinners included the foods of the Middle East and the foods of Spain.

On the main floor of the inn is the lounge-library with its wide-ranging selection of reading material and the Cabaret, a large room open evenings as a showcase for a variety of performers selected by Marantz from all over the East Coast, including singers, mimes, one-person shows, and improvisational theater groups. Eventually the two barns on the property will be renovated and will house the performing arts center and the visual arts center.

The second floor guest rooms are individually decorated with a blend of authentic antiques and colonial-style furniture. Most rooms have private baths although some share bath facilities. Each has a view of either the mountains or the Battenkill. There is also a "honeymoon cottage" with full housekeeping facilities and a fireplace. Rooms may be rented on a weekly basis, often to parties of trout fishermen, in a detached duplex apartment. The inn has a stable with horses and, in winter, 10 miles of cross-country skiing on marked trails on the property as well as access to the adjoining state land. *Room Rates*: $18 to $30 plus $7 per person additional per room; MAP, $10 per person, daily. Pets are permitted if special advance arrangements are made. *Driving Instructions*: The inn is two miles west of the village of Arlington on Route 313. Arlington is located on Route 7 north of Bennington.

Brandon, Vermont

In addition to being an excellent base for fishermen because of its location on the Neshobe River, the area has good cross-country skiing. It is a short drive to the south to the *Proctor Marble Exhibit*, just outside of Rutland, and *Brandon Brook Recreational Area* is only a few miles to the east of Brandon on Route 73, as is *Chittenden Brook Recreational Area*. These areas are parts of the U.S. Forest Service system and offer picnicking and fishing. Chittenden Brook has campsites and trailer facilities as well.

CHURCHILL HOUSE INN

Route 73 East. Brandon VT. Mailing Address: RFD #3, Brandon, VT 05733. 802-247-3300. *Innkeepers:* Michael and Marion Shonstrom. Oper all year except April 1 to May 15 and November 1 to December 15.

The Churchill House is an impressive three-story farmhouse built in 1871 by the Churchill family from local lumber. Mike and Marion Shonstrom have managed to furnish the house with a large collection of antiques supplemented by a few contemporary furnishings. There are high bedsteads of maple, oak, and cast iron; commodes; and blanket chests, as well as parlor and Franklin stoves in the downstairs sitting room and the book-lined study.

Food here is a product of the hard work of Marion, who loves provincial cooking, be it Vermont style or with a continental flare. Some of her specialties include pot roast simmered in cranberry-

and-horseradish sauce, roast lamb with yogurt and barley pilaf, and chicken Provençal. The proprietors grow their own vegetables in the warmer months, and they also bake their own very fine French bread.

The inn has several special package plans that will appeal to travelers in every season. It offers, in the spring, early summer, and fall a special series of fly-fishing programs. Because the inn is located on the Neshobe River and has easy access to local beaver ponds, lakes, and other rivers, it has become a gathering place for fly fishermen. During these periods the inn offers special fly-fishing clinics, including fly-tying and casting instruction. The inn also offers five-day guided tours using canoes and led by local guide Scott Rideout. Each such tour costs $175. Fishermen who prefer to be on their own can arrange through the Churchill House fishing tours that use other inns as the base camps. Other participating inns are the Tulip Tree Inn in Chittenden and the 1811 House in Manchester.

Bicyclists will enjoy the variety of bicycle tours organized by this inn, which include evening stops at several inns on trips that range in length from two- or three-day tours to a grand tour of seven days and two hundred miles. Besides the Churchill House, nine inns are described in the brochure available from the Shonstroms.

Hikers will enjoy a similar program called "Hike Inn to Inn," which is co-organized by the Churchill House Inn and the Tulip Tree Inn in Chittenden. Write to either for details.

The Churchill House Inn maintains a complete ski-touring center with 22 miles of cross-country trails, as well as a ski shop with rentals, instruction, and guided tours available. The inn participates in a winter program of ski touring that links several old country inns in a manner similar to the bicycling and hiking programs mentioned above.

Room Rates: $25 to $30 per person, MAP, based on double occupancy. Tax and 15 percent gratuity are added to all bills. *Driving Instructions:* Take Route 7 to Brandon, then route 73 east to the inn.

Brownsville, Vermont (Mount Ascutney)
Mount Ascutney is a small ski area near the Connecticut River in

the western part of central Vermont. The mountain is adjacent to the village of Brownsville. The ski area has two chair and three T-bar lifts serving 24 trails and 4 slopes. There are also several miles of marked cross-country ski trails at Mount Ascutney. In the summer, the mountain is a popular gathering spot for climbers.

THE INN AT MOUNT ASCUTNEY

Brook Road, Brownsville, VT 05037. 802-484-5997. *Innkeeper*: Daphne Henderson. Open all year except for two weeks in April and two weeks in November.

The Inn at Mount Ascutney is a 150-year-old country inn with simple rooms. Fireplaces blaze in the living and dining rooms and candles and lamps provide the only light during dinner. Cooking is done on an open hearth in the dining room. The inn has long been famous for its views of Mount Ascutney both by day and—thanks to lights for night skiing—by evening. Mrs. Henderson, a graduate of the Cordon Bleu School of Cooking, is an accomplished chef. Nightly she offers a continental menu with seven appetizers including escargots and stuffed mushrooms and seven entrees including duck à l'orange, fresh salmon with Béarnaise sauce, veal scallopini marsala, and coquilles St. Jacques. Dinner prices are a la carte with entrees averaging $8. *Room Rates*: Single rooms, $14; double rooms, $12 per person. Breakfast included. Some pets are permitted. *Driving Instructions*: Take either Route 44 from Windsor to the east or Route 106 to the west. When at Brownsville, take Brook Road to the inn.

Chester, Vermont (including Gassetts)

Chester is a quiet, unspoiled town in southeastern Vermont. It is convenient to a number of ski areas including *Magic Mountain*, *Timber Ridge*, and *Okemo* to mention only the three closest. Nearby Springfield has several tourist attractions including the *Eureka School*, the first school built in Vermont (1785). Near the school is one of Vermont's many covered bridges. Springfield also houses the *Springfield Art and Historical Society*. The *Old Stone Village* at Chester, is a fine collection of old houses and a church all built of stone. In town, too, are the Chester Art Guild, the Grist Mill, the Green Mountain Railroad's Steam Train Terminal.

THE OLD TOWNE FARM LODGE

Route 10, Gassetts, VT. Mailing Address: RFD #1, Chester Depot, VT 05144. 802-875-2346. *Innkeepers*: Fred and Jan Baldwin and family. Open all year except Thanksgiving Day.

This large white farmhouse is noted for a handmade spiral staircase that is a real testimony to early craftsmanship. The lodge has nine guest rooms, two with private baths. The remainder share three bathrooms. There are wide board floors throughout and the rooms are partially furnished with antiques.

The farm was originally built more than a century ago and known as the Chester "Town Farm." The indigent of the town were given food and lodging in return for a hard day's work on the farm. The property was sold by the town in the 1950s and was operated as a farm for a while before being converted by its owners into an inn. The inn then changed hands and was more completely renovated in the early 1970s. The current owners, the Baldwin family, purchased the inn in July 1977.

The inn has a spring-fed pond for swimming, fishing, and skating. It is heated by a huge wood furnace and the fragrance of wood smoke greets travelers on the approach to the inn during the winter months. Meals are simple and substantial; they feature items like breast of chicken with cranberry glaze, roast beef, sirloin steak, lasagne, and Jan Baldwin's special homemade desserts. *Room Rates*: $8.50 to $20 per person, MAP. Rates are half price for children under 13 staying in parents' room. Pets are permitted. *Driving Instructions*: I-91 to exit 6. Route 103 north through Chester to Route 10. Turn right on Route 10. Drive ½ mile to the inn.

Chittenden, Vermont

Chittenden is a small village on the edge of the Green Mountain National forest. The area is quiet and has several country inns as well as a few larger resorts nearby. Neighboring Rutland and Practor offer the tourist a number of special attractions including *Wilson's Castle*, a nineteenth-century mansion; the marble exhibit at the *Vermont Marble Company*; the *Chaffee Art Gallery*; and the Rutland *Historical Society Museum*. Area skiing includes well-organized cross-country skiing at several inns, as well as other trails and downhill skiing at *Apple Hill, Pico and Killington*. Golf is available at the *Proctor-Pittsford Golf Course*.

TULIP TREE INN

> Chittenden, VT 05737. 802-483-6213. *Innkeepers*: Barbara and Gerald Liebert. Open all year.

For years the Lieberts had visited New England inns for vacations. Finally, one year, they purchased a rambling, turn of the century country home and used all their skills to renovate and redecorate it in time to welcome their first guests to Christmas at the Tulip Tree. Business has been wonderful ever since at this inn, described by many as being the most fun inn in Vermont. It is relaxed and happy, giving one the feeling of being a family house guest. There are only nine guest rooms with five shared or connecting baths. This inn is particularly popular during cross-country skiing season when it is part of a "ski from inn to inn" plan that connects several popular area inns. Most of the cooking is done by Mrs. Liebert and is representative of several cuisines, all excellent. Thus, many diners lodging elsewhere will make a special effort to eat at the Tulip Tree. Among the favorite dishes are homemade paté, veal piccata, chicken in phyllo and an assortment of unusual desserts. *Room Rates*: $23 to $26 per person, MAP, plus gratuities. No pets permitted. *Driving Instructions*: The inn is located in Chittenden on a country road north of Rutland. Take Route 4 east of Rutland and watch for signs to Chittenden.

Dorset, Vermont

Dorset is a quiet village of great beauty in all seasons and has been a favorite of artists for many years. It was the location of the first *marble quarry* in the state, now a favorite swimming area. More swimming and boating are available at nearby *Emerald Lake*. Tennis and golf can be enjoyed at the *Dorset Field Club*. One of Vermont's famed summer theaters, the *Dorset Playhouse*, operates here. Four great ski centers, *Bromley*, *Stratton*, *Magic Mountain*, and *Snow Valley* are all within easy driving distance. Trout fishing in the Battenkill River and deer hunting in the forests make the area popular with these sports' lovers as well.

BARROWS HOUSE

Dorset, VT 05251. 802-867-4455. *Innkeepers*: Charles and Marilyn Schubert. Open all year.

Barrows House is actually a collection of buildings in the heart of Dorset. The inn property includes several old buildings, all carefully renovated and redecorated by the Schuberts, which offer a variety of types of accommodations from singles to large families. The buildings are all named and include Barrows House, Hemlock House, Truffle House, a Carriage House (once an old forge), Birds Nest, and the Stable. Here the visitor will find rooms of all sizes and styles, with several suites available. Larger families can stay in the Truffle House where they can share three twin-bedded rooms and a common living room with fireplace. The Stable has rooms with old exposed beams and is the most expensive. Most rooms have wall-to-wall carpeting and many have coordinated drapes, quilts, and wallpaper.

The tavern at the inn is decorated with oak furniture. All meals are served under the careful supervision of the young talented

cook, Sissy. First hired as a chambermaid, she quickly made her talent as a chef and supervisor of kitchen help known and is now the driving force behind the inn's recent boom in popularity as a Dorset dining spot.

Recreational facilities at Barrows House are excellent. Many cross-country skiers start right at their door (rentals are available) and the inn has its own swimming pool and tennis courts for warm weather use. There is a gazebo for relaxing at the end of a warm Vermont summer day. Badminton and croquet are popular here in the summer and fall. Golfing at the Dorset Field Club and horseback riding are available in the immediate vicinity. *Room Rates*: Single rooms, $22 to $30, MAP; double rooms $50 to $60, MAP. In addition, there is a 15 percent gratuities charge plus 5 percent Vermont state tax. *Driving Instructions*: From Route 7 in Vermont take Route 30 northeast to Dorset. Route 30 leaves Route 7 just north of Manchester.

DORSET INN

Church and Main Streets, Dorset, VT 05251. Mailing Address: Box 8, Dorset, VT 05251. 802-867-5500. *Innkeeper*: Gred G. Russell. Open from late May to late October and from late December to late March.

The Dorset Inn was built in two sections. The first section, dating from 1796, makes it the state's oldest inn; the second, built in 1850, now houses the living room and dining room. The inn is characterized by quaint, old-fashioned decorations including wide board floors and fourposter beds, antiques and more recent solid country furniture. Most of the 47 rooms have been renovated to include private baths, although 7 share baths.

The inn has a swimming pool, and it is within easy walking distance of Vermont's oldest nine-hole golf course at the Dorset Field Club. Cookouts are held every Thursday night in the warmer months. The dining room has an intimate feeling with its papered walls and simple curtained windows. Meals are described as "authentic New England menus, prepared to delicious Yankee perfection." The dinner menu is kept small and includes four or five simple selections like steak, chicken, or haddock with appetizer, salad, and dessert included in the dinner price which ranges from $4.50 to $6.75 with a surcharge to inn guests for certain of the more expensive items. *Room Rates*: Single rooms, $23 to $29, MAP; doubles, $35 to $37 or $39 to $43 with twin beds, MAP. A 15 percent surcharge for gratuities is added. Pets are permitted. *Driving Instructions*: From Route 7 in Vermont take Route 30 northeast to Dorset. Rt. 30 leaves Rt. 7 just north of Manchester.

Hartland, Vermont

Hartland is a small town on the Connecticut River, eight miles north of Windsor. The town has no special sightseeing or recreational facilities but is near the many sights of Windsor which include the historic *Constitution House*, where the Vermont State Constitution was first framed. The *American Precision Museum* offers a fine collection of machines, tools, and their products. There is golf at the *Windsor Country Club* and skiing at the *Mount Ascutney Ski Area*. A fine covered bridge crosses the Connecticut River here. There are several river-powered mills in this area open to the public.

CADY BROOK FARM

Jenneville Road, Hartland, VT 05048. Mailing Address: RR 1, Box 120, Windsor, VT 05089. 802-436-2486. *Innkeepers*: Ruth and John Sammel. Open all year.

The Cady Brook Farm offers families a chance to stay in a small, remote 1794 Federal-style building which has been renovated recently but retains the feeling of its original period. It was built by an officer who served in the Revolutionary War. The inn was then known as Burkes Stand and was a stop on the stagecoach route between Woodstock and Windsor. Some of its rooms have had the paint removed to reveal original stenciling. There are only four guest rooms and these all share bath facilities.

Meals are served family style and feature simple home cooking. *Room Rates*: For adults, $15 per day or $80 per week per person, MAP. Lower rates for children. Pets are permitted. *Driving Instructions*: The inn is rather remote and located on a country dirt road. Guests who make reservations are sent a special map.

Landgrove, Vermont

Landgrove is a tiny town in the Green Mountain National Forest, about 15 miles northeast of Manchester. The town is served by unpaved country roads only. However, it is a short drive to the neighboring towns of Weston and Peru (both of which are interesting to visit) as well as Londonderry.

THE VILLAGE INN

RFD Landgrove, VT 05148. 802-824-6673. *Innkeeper*: D. Jay Snyder. Open from December 1 through April 15 and from July 1 through October 15.

The first part of the Village Inn was constructed in 1810 and has had various additions over the years. The most recent was made in 1976. The result is a series of low interconnected buildings, mostly in clapboard, that has come to serve as a small resort rather than a strictly country inn. On the property are a private tennis court, a heated outdoor pool, and a nine-hole pitch-and-putt course. Inn guests who enjoy cross-country skiing can use trails that originate there, while downhill skiers have only short drives to Bromley, Stratton, Magic Mountain, Snow Valley, or Okemo. There is a Rafter Room Lounge (bring your own bottle) to entertain folks who enjoy that sort of thing. (Guests here can enjoy the combination of rural seclusion and some resort facilities.) The rooms are large, with curtains, comforters, and an old-fashioned look. Dinners at the inn are simple affairs featuring such main courses as roast beef with Bordelaise sauce or chicken Kiev. Desserts include carrot

cake, coffee mousse pie, apple knobby cake, and apple crisp. *Room Rates*: In winter, double rooms with private bath, $23 to $26 per person, MAP; rooms without bath are less expensive. Summer rates are EP but were not available at the time of publication. No pets permitted. *Driving Instructions*: From Manchester take Route 11 past Bromley Ski Area and turn left into Peru village. At the folk in Peru bear left and continue 4½ miles through the National Forest to the crossroads in Landgrove. Turn left toward Weston; the inn is on the right.

Londonderry, Vermont

Londonderry is located in south central Vermont at the edge of the Green Mountain National Forest. Nearby is *Magic Mountain Ski Area* with its 22 trails and 3 slopes served by a total of 5 lifts. The immensely popular *Stratton Mountain* has 10 lifts that serve 59 miles of trails. This is a huge, year-round resort with hundreds of nonskiing activities including pools, saunas, indoor tennis, and ice skating.

NORDIC INN

Route 11, Londonderry, VT 05148. 802-824-6444. *Innkeepers*: Inger Johansson and Filippo Pagano. Open from Thanksgiving until the end of the ski season and then from Memorial Day through the fall foliage season.

The Nordic Inn is a converted New England residence that now houses a small inn steeped in Swedish tradition. The interior is decorated with Scandinavian antiques, many of which were brought here from the Johansson family farm in Kisa, Sweden. The inn has five guest rooms named Sweden, Norway, Finland, Denmark, and Vermont. Each room is painted in the colors of that country's (or state's) flag. There are two intimate dining rooms with fireplaces and views of the surrounding landscape, as well as a cosy cocktail lounge with a pub atmosphere including two dart boards. The inn is a local dart center with tournaments and a dart shop. The lounge has a roaring fire in cold weather. The inn is noted for its Scandinavian cuisine prepared under the strict supervision of Inger Johansson, a professional chef who was head chef for the consul general of Sweden and, later, assistant manager of Corporate Food Services for RCA at Rockefeller Center. The menu is an extensive one, including such popular Scandinavian specialties as smorrebrod, gravad lax med sas, liver paté, salmon baked on a bed of dill, veal scallops a la Oscar, and a special chicken breast. Desserts are continental and include mocha crepe, Danish rum pudding, and apples baked in almond butter and cream and topped with lingonberries.

The inn is particularly noted as a cross-country ski base with eight miles of marked and groomed trails. Equipment rentals and instruction are available. This center is open to both guests at the inn and to the general public. *Room Rates*: In winter, $21.50 to $28.50 per person, MAP; in summer, $8 to $10 per person, EP. Highest rates are for a room with private bath and fireplace. *Driving Instructions*: The inn is located west of Londonderry in the Landgrove region on Route 11.

Manchester Village, Vermont

Manchester has long drawn both summer and winter visitors to this mountainous area. Nearby are the *Big Bromley* and *Stratton Mountain* ski areas. During the warmer months, there is a spectacular *Equinox Skyline Drive* to the top of Mount Equinox (toll road). Those who fish will certainly enjoy stopping at the *American Museum of Fly Fishing* and also at the headquarters of the Orvis Company, fly rod manufacturers. The *Southern Vermont Art Center* has a collection of paintings, graphics, and sculpture. Nearby *Emerald Lake State Park* is located to the north of the village on U.S. Route 7. Also in Manchester is a branch of *Basketville*.

RELUCTANT PANTHER INN

West Road (just off Route 7), Manchester Village, VT 05254. 802-362-2568. *Innkeepers*: Mr. and Mrs. Stephen W. Cornell III. Open December 24 through Easter and Memorial Day through October 30.

The Reluctant Panther was fashioned out of an imposing clapboard home built in 1850. The inn has 7 guest rooms, several with

89

working fireplaces. The décor in all the rooms is varied but very stylish. Wall-to-wall carpets are the rule.

The two dining rooms (one is a solarium with a glass ceiling), are open to the public and are considered to be among the finest in the area. All dinners are price fixed with rates for a complete meal at $10 to $14. The menu includes two cold soups, avgolemone and gazpacho; two hot soups, carrot top and green pea; four hors d'oeuvres including a tiny broiled trout and bacon-wrapped asparagus. There are nine carefully prepared entrees including crepes, filet of beef Wellington, and veal Cordon Bleu, among others. *Room Rates*: $25 to $35 for a double room with private bath. No young children or pets permitted. *Driving Instructions*: The inn is located in the center of Manchester Village about 20 miles north of Bennington on Route 7.

Marlboro, Vermont

Marlboro is a quiet college town in the southeastern portion of Vermont about 10 miles west of Brattleboro. It is best known for the *Marlboro Music Festival* held each summer under the direction of Rudolf Serkin. Winter visitors to this area are within easy driving of downhill ski areas—Hogback, Haystack, and Mount Snow.

WHETSTONE INN

Marlboro, VT 05344. 802-254-2500. *Innkeepers*: Mr. and Mrs. Hubert Moore. Open all year.

The Whetstone Inn, situated at the top of a hill, was built in 1785 and was first used as a tavern in stagecoach days. The public rooms have cheery fires and an ample supply of interesting books, records, and games. The Moores, who have been innkeepers for a number of years, are most hospitable and the inn is inviting in all seasons. In winter there is cross-country skiing, sledding, and snowshoeing right on the inn's grounds, and downhill skiing available a short distance away. Warmer weather finds visitors enjoying hiking or photography or taking part in activities on the campus of Marlboro College, two miles away.

The 10 guest rooms are large and well appointed. Most have fourposter beds and 5 have private baths. Only breakfast is served at the inn. *Room Rates*: Single rooms, $13; double rooms, $22 to $26. Breakfast included. Pets are permitted with advance notice. *Driving Instructions:* From Route I-91, take exit 2 (Brattleboro) and go 8½ miles west on Route 9, then ½ mile south into the village of Marlboro.

Mendon, Vermont

Mendon is a small town a few miles outside Rutland, the second largest city in Vermont. Despite its closeness to a rather developed area it remains a rural town that enjoys breathtaking views of the surrounding mountain peaks. Fine area skiing exists at the nearby Killington, Pico, and Apple Hill Ski areas. There is ample cross-country skiing in winter, and hiking in the warmer months. The *Marble Exhibit* in Proctor and *Wilson Castle*, a restored nineteenth-century mansion in Rutland, are short drives away.

VERMONT INN

Route 4, Mendon, VT 05701. 802-773-9847. *Innkeepers*: Judy and Alan Carmasin. Open year round.

The Vermont Inn was originally a farmhouse built in the early nineteenth century. The small inn, recently redecorated, has 13 rooms, most with shared, central baths. The views from the inn of Killington, Pico, and Shrewsbury Peaks are spectacular. It is part of a guided, inn-to-inn cross-country ski tour that starts at the Tulip Tree Inn in Chittenden (write them for details). The lovely dining room, with its picture windows and fieldstone fireplace, serves dinners ranging from $3.95 to $8.50. House specialties include baked stuffed jumbo shrimp, veal piccata, and Vermont turkey pie. *Room Rates*: From $16 per person for a dormitory room (for five or six people); from $17 per person for double room with shared bath; $22 per person for double room with private bath. *Driving Instructions*: Take Route 4 five miles east of Rutland or four miles west of Killington.

Newfane, Vermont

Newfane is a small town that houses a particularly fine pillared Federal-style *Courthouse* built in 1825. This much photographed village is within easy drive of the *Townshend State Forest* and a small ski area known as *Maple Valley*, which is in nearby West Dummerston. Also within driving distance are Brattleboro and Marlboro with its famous summer music festival. Auctions are held in Newfane every Saturday night in the summer.

THE FOUR COLUMNS INN

230 West Street, Newfane, VT 05345. 802-365-7713. *Innkeeper*: René Chardain. Open from late May to November and from late December to April. The restaurant of this inn is closed on Mondays.

The Four Columns Inn houses one of the more distinguished French restaurants in New England, awarded three stars in the Mobil Guide. The inn consists of a white clapboard building with its four columns and a red clapboard barn that serves as the restaurant. Here the specialties vary according to season and include salmon a l'oseille, scampi, guinea hen, and pheasant. The restaurant also serves fresh trout and the traditional duck a l'orange as well as an assortment of dishes prepared in classic French ways. Prices vary according to the seasonal selections and are generally quite expensive. Luncheon is not served in the winter.

The inn has 12 guest rooms featuring spool beds. All rooms have private baths. *Room Rates*: $28 to $40. Pets are permitted. *Driving Instructions*: The inn is 100 yards off Route 30 in the center of Newfane.

OLD NEWFANE INN

Route 30 and the Common, Newfane, VT 05345. 802-365-4427. *Innkeeper*: Eric Weindl. Open from May to October and December to April.

Not far from the Four Columns is a fine old Vermont inn with an impressive menu. Built in 1787, the Old Newfane is filled with early American antiques and retains the wide board floors, beamed ceilings, and red brick fireplaces characteristic of this period. It was built on Newfane Hill and moved to the present location on the Common in 1825. The extensive and not inexpensive French menu in the dining room lists over a dozen appetizers and even more entrees, including specialties such as medallion de veau aux champignons, frogs' legs Provençale, rack of lamb, duckling l'orange, and veal Gismonda. The 10 papered guest rooms are decorated in traditional old New England style. Eight of the rooms have private baths; the remaining two have a connecting bath. This inn, like the Four Columns, is highly recommended to travelers who wish excellent food in a somewhat formal atmosphere. *Room Rates*: Double rooms, $35 to $45. No children or pets are permitted. *Driving Instructions*: Take Route 30 to Newfane. The inn is in the center of town.

Peru, Vermont

Peru is a small village which serves as a less hectic base for the enjoyment of *Big Bromley Ski Area* (and its summer alpine slide).

Cross-country skiers enjoy nearby *Viking Ski Center* and *Wild Wings*. Vacationers seeking other forms of entertainment and sightseeing are encouraged to drive to neighboring Manchester and Manchester Center as well as to Londonderry to the east. At Londonderry, Route 11 joins Route 100, which meanders through some of Vermont's most beautiful scenery. Hiking along the Appalachian Trail and fishing in the Battenkill River are among some of the warm weather pleasures available here. Also located in Peru is the *Hapgood Recreation Area* which offers picnicking, camping, boating, swimming, and hiking. A short drive away is Weston, with its numerous year-round attractions.

JOHNNY SEESAW'S

Route 11, Peru, VT 05012. 802-824-5533. *Innkeepers*: Larry and Anne Ward, Sarah and Tony McKim. Open July 4 through foliage season and Thanksgiving through the end of the snow season.

The original building of this inn dates from 1926 as a dance hall, but it has been renovated and made larger since then. At one point, several cottages were added so that guests now may choose a country inn atmosphere or the greater privacy offered by the cottages, which all have private baths, fireplaces in the living rooms, and television. The inn has private guest rooms, bunk rooms, a dining room, and the main living room with its round fireplace. Guests frequently gather around the fire in the raised alcove to relax and sing to guitar music. The inn has its own swimming pool and tennis court for summer use.

Dinners at the inn are examples of simple country cooking—homemade soups, breads, desserts, and pies highlight the meal. Children are often served early to allow their parents to enjoy a more leisurely meal. After dinner the children may retire to their own private television room complete with pinball machine. *Room Rates*: All rates are per person, MAP. In the cottages, $32; in the inn with private bath, $24 to $29; with shared bath, $22. Rates for bunk room and for children (ages 7–14) are less. Pets are permitted. *Driving Instructions*: Take Route 7 to Route 11 east. Peru is midway between Manchester and Londonderry.

WILEY INN

Route 11, Peru, VT 05152. 802-824-6600. *Innkeeper*: Grace Tarplin. Open all year except for November and from April 15 to June 15.

The Wiley is a 100-year-old inn located on Bromley Mountain in the heart of some of Vermont's finest ski areas. The inn is small and cosy and features regional cooking supervised by a former New York caterer with 25 years of experience. There are two lounges with fireplaces and 18 guest rooms, 8 with baths and 10 with shared baths. Summer guests swim in the inn's heated pool and drive to nearby hiking, golf, tennis, and other recreational and sightseeing activities.

Dining is available for both guests and the public at breakfast and dinner. Specialties include chicken crepe divan, baked ham-cheese élegant, Bavarian pot roast, and rock cornish hen marsala; all are accompanied by special baked breads and potato or rice dishes. *Room Rates*: In winter, rooms with private baths, $25 per person, MAP. Rooms with shared baths cost less. Summer rates are not yet available but are expected to start at $10 per person, including breakfast. *Driving Instructions*: Take Route 7 to Route 22 and then into Peru.

Plymouth Notch, Vermont

Plymouth was the scene of a gold rush many years ago, and over $2 million in gold was taken from the area. Even today, gold is occasionally panned from local rivers. However, Plymouth is best known as the birthplace of President Calvin Coolidge. The *Calvin Coolidge National Historical Restoration* and his family birthplace-homestead is here. It was here that he became the only President to be sworn in by his own father. The *Plymouth Cheese Factory*, run by Coolidge's son, is open to the public; visitors can watch the cheese being made. Skiing is available at the *Round Top Ski Area*, with its two chair lifts. Seven miles away is the *Killington Ski Area* with its famous gondola and the longest ski season in the east. Near the Coolidge homestead is the *Wilder House*, birthplace of Coolidge's mother and now a visitors center. *Wilder Barn*, in the village, houses a fine museum of farming tools and related farm implements.

SALT ASH INN

Junction of Routes 100 and 100A, Plymouth Union, VT 05056. 802 672-3748. *Innkeepers:* Don and Ginny Kroitzsh. Open in the summer, fall, and winter.

The Salt Ash Inn has had a rich history as, at various times, a stagecoach stop, post office, inn, and general store. Most of the antiques in the building were originally used there. A large circular fireplace warms the lounge and there is also a small pub. The old post office boxes still remain. You can even see President Coolidge's name on the box where he picked up his mail years ago. The twelve guest rooms are cheerful and retain the flavor of the past. Most have private or connecting baths and all have wall-to-wall carpeting and quilts on the beds. Food is served family

style with home-baked bread and a salad bar. The inn serves both breakfast and dinner to guests and the public. *Room Rates*: During peak season times, $15 to $22 per person, MAP. At other times, $7 to $10 per person, EP. No pets permitted. *Driving Instructions*: Junction of Routes 100 and 100A.

Proctorsville and Ludlow, Vermont

These towns are adjacent to *Okemo Mountain* with its somewhat more relaxed ski area featuring three double chair lifts and six Poma lifts. There are smaller ski school classes and shorter lift lines than at some of Vermont's major areas. This is one of the most popular areas for family skiing in Vermont. In Ludlow, the *Black River Academy Museum* houses local artifacts. Calvin Coolidge was an 1890 graduate of the Academy. The Okemo Winter Carnival is held in Ludlow in mid-January each year. Visitors may purchase samples of two of Vermont's major food products at the *Crowley Cheese Shop* and the *Green Mountain Sugar House*.

GOLDEN STAGE INN

Route 103, Proctorsville, VT 05153. 802-226-7744. Mailing Address: P.O. Box 218, Proctorsville, VT 05153. *Innkeepers*: Tom and Wende Schaaff. Open all year. Dining room is open daily except Mondays.

Built in 1796, the Golden Stage has been a stagecoach stop and private home for 180 years. The inn was once a link in the underground railroad; much later it was the home of Cornelia Otis Skinner. It has had only six owners in its long history and has been completely redone by the Schaaffs. The inn is a rambling clapboard building with wrap-around porches and attached barn set on four acres of rolling lawns and gardens. Summer visitors often lounge on one of the porches and take in the view.

There are eight guest rooms, only one with a private bath; the others share bath facilities. A barn-board paneled lounge with a copper bar and fireplace, a library, and a large plant-filled room with another fireplace provide plenty of space for guests to relax. The dining room (open to the public with advance reservations) serves traditional New England dishes as well as continental cuisine. The menu features homemade soups, crepes, and quiches.

The inn utilizes produce from their own garden during the summer season. Breakfast, lunch, and dinner are served. *Room Rates*: In winter, $25 per person, MAP. In summer, $20 per person, with only breakfast included. There are also special five-day winter ski packages. No pets permitted. *Driving Instructions*: Take Route 91 to exit 6, then north on Route 103, 16 miles to the inn.

Quechee, Vermont

Quechee is a small town that is currently going through a good deal of expansion due to the development efforts of the Quechee Lakes Corporation, which has bought 5500 acres here and is developing about half of them. Quechee is located between the towns of Woodstock and White River Junction on Route 4, approximately six miles from the Connecticut River.

QUECHEE INN

Marshland Farm, Clubhouse Road, Quechee, VT 05059. Mailing Address: Box 457, Quechee, VT 05059. 802-295-3133. *Innkeeper:* Craig Taylor; owner Quechee Lakes Corporation. Open year round.

Colonel Joseph Marsh, the first lieutenant governor of Vermont, built his home, known as Marshland, in 1793, using timber he had transported from Connecticut. The stately building was the home of the Marshes for many years. In 1971 the mansion, in almost perfect condition, was purchased and restored by the Quechee Lakes Corporation, which was developing 5500 acres of nearby land into a private village with a multimillion-dollar clubhouse and recreation complex. The corporation opened the inn to guests in 1975, offering accommodations in the restored building completely furnished with antiques. The inn has a public lounge with a fireplace. No meals are served except for a continental breakfast for guests only. All guests have access to the wide range of recreational facilities at the Quechee Lakes including 18-hole golf, tennis, paddleball, squash, saunas, and a private ski area with a 2700-foot double chair lift. *Room Rates*: $32 for standard room; $38, deluxe. No pets permitted. *Driving Instructions*: Clubhouse Road is 1½ miles west on Route 4 from I-89.

Tyson, Vermont (see Proctorsville and Ludlow)

ECHO LAKE INN

Route 100, Tyson, VT. Mailing Address: Box 142, Ludlow, VT 05149. 802-226-8602. *Manager*: Roger Scully; owners: Dennis and Barbara Scully. Open all year except for short closings in late fall and spring.

The Echo Lake Inn was first built in 1800 and additions were made in 1869. It has always been either an inn or a hotel. The entire building was fully refurbished in 1971–72 and it is currently decorated and furnished with reproductions of country antiques. The inn has a somewhat formal atmosphere, suitable to a lodging of its size (21 guest rooms). It is situated on Echo Lake and provides guests with a dock full of canoes and rowboats. There is lake swimming at the sandy beach nearby or guests may use the inn's heated swimming pool. Other facilities include an all-weather tennis court with lights for nighttime play and the inn's own ice skating rink across the street. Adjacent to the inn is an early cheese factory that has been converted to an antique and gift shop; many of the interesting structural features of this old building have been retained. *Room Rates*: Double rooms with private baths, $27; with connecting bath, $22; with baths in hall, $18. Pets are permitted in certain special cases only. *Driving Instructions*: The inn is five miles north of Ludlow on Route 100.

West Dover, Vermont

West Dover is a small village in south central Vermont noted primarily for its proximity to three ski areas, *Mount Snow, Carinthia*, and *Haystack*. Mount Snow is one of Vermont's most popular ski resorts and the *Mount Snow Country Club* offers golf, tennis, and horseback riding, among other things, in the summer months. Summer visitors can enjoy the concerts at the *Marlboro Music Festival*, described in the volume on sightseeing. Also nearby are the villages of Wilmington, Newfane, and Wardsboro.

THE HANDLE HOUSE

Handle Road, West Dover, VT 05356. 802-464-5449. *Innkeeper*: Winifred Sargent. Open Dec.–April, July–Aug.

Once a stagecoach stop in the Revolutionary days, the Handle House is now a farm-inn with eight guest rooms, all with private baths. The inn has an active summer program for the children of guests including swimming, riding (using the farm stables), archery, sailing, and tennis. Many neighborhood children also participate in the camplike atmosphere. Riding is available for adults as well. In winter, skiing takes over—either downhill at neighboring Mount Snow or Haystack or cross-country, from the doorstep of the inn. Breakfast and dinner are served to guests only. Typical dinner selections might include roast prime ribs of beef or beef Bourguignon. The inn's special programs make it particularly suitable for families with young children. *Room Rates*: $22 per person, MAP. *Driving Instructions*: The inn is located near Route 100 north of West Dover. A map is sent to guests when they make their advance reservations.

INN AT SAWMILL FARM

Route 100, West Dover, VT 05356. 802-464-8131. Mailing Address: Box 8, West Dover, VT 05356. *Innkeeper:* Rodney C. Williams. Open all year except November 15 to December 1.

This 1779 property has undergone a renovation which has completely transformed the interior of the buildings into facilities with modern conveniences, while still retaining the old Vermont feeling. The buildings use the original structure with exposed beams and time-softened barn board in an extremely effective way. Combined with a highly acclaimed kitchen, the reconstruction has made the Inn at Sawmill Farm one of the most respected inns in the state. Many of the guest rooms and suites have fireplaces for added comfort. The inn is filled with brass, copper, and other antiques. There is a pond on the property which provides swimming and trout fishing in the summer and skating in the winter.

The restaurant, with its exposed timbers and old mill tools on display, features an impressive array of dishes. Appetizers include Irish smoked salmon, coquille of lobster, escargots, and their famed Vermont appetizer—asparagus tips wrapped in ham and baked with Vermont cheddar cheese. Dinner entrees include scallopini a l'Anglaise, roast duck poivre vert, frogs legs Provençale, and breast of chicken with white wine and black olives. The dessert menu includes chocolate cake, cheese cake, a special chocolate sundae, and homemade pies. Dinners are a la carte, and full dinners would range in price from about $12.50 to $18.50 per person. *Room Rates:* Double rooms, $80 for two, MAP; fireplace suites, $90 to $100 for two, MAP. No pets permitted. *Driving Instructions:* I-91 to Brattleboro. Then take Route 9 west 21 miles to Wilmington. Take Route 100 north five miles to the inn. From the New York Thruway, exit at Troy and follow Route 7 east to Bennington, then take Route 9 to Wilmington and continue as above.

West Townshend, Vermont

West Townshend is located at the edge of the Green Mountain National Forest and is characterized by rolling hills and deep valleys. *Townshend Lake* has swimming, boating, and fishing and the *Townshend State Forest* has facilities for hiking, bird watching, swimming, fishing and camping. The *Windham Heights Country Club*, eight miles to the north, has tennis, golf, and swimming available. West Townshend is within 10 to 15 miles of several downhill ski areas including *Mount Snow, Carinthia, Timber Ridge*, and *Magic Mountain*. There are seven ski-touring centers in the general vicinity.

WINDHAM HILL FARM

West Townshend, VT 05359. 802-874-5951. *Innkeeper*: Hugh C. Folsom. Open from May to October and December to April.

The Windham Hill Farm is a small country inn in a carefully restored 135-year-old farmhouse on a hill overlooking the local mountains and the West River Valley. The inn has deliberately been kept small to maintain its informal atmosphere. Innkeeper Hugh Folsom said recently, "Our guests are, for the most part, quite self-sufficient and do not need or participate in organized activities. They're content with back roads, trails, swimming holes, waterfalls, flowers, birds, and wildlife rather than tennis courts and golf courses. They listen to the frogs in our pond rather than canned music from a radio." This does, indeed, produce the effect of being a house guest rather than a transient.

Meals are served by candlelight. Summer dinners include food raised in the inn's large, organic garden. There is no set menu so

that the freshest in-season foods can be used. The public is welcome at dinner with advance reservations. *Room Rates*: $23 to $26 per person per day, or $138 to $156 per person per week, based on double occupancy, MAP. Single occupancy rates are higher. No pets permitted. *Driving Instructions*: From Brattleboro, 21 miles northwest on Route 30 to West Townshend. Turn right, up Windham Road, 1¼ miles to inn sign on the right-hand side.

West Wardsboro, Vermont

West Wardsboro is five miles north of Mount Snow and is a winter stopping place for visitors to that famous ski area who do not wish to be in the middle of activities at the ski center or in the busier West Dover. The area has numerous cross-country ski trails. Summer visitors often hike along *The Long Trail*, which passes nearby. Recreational facilities are numerous in all seasons, especially at *Mount Snow*.

THE GREEN MOUNTAIN HOUSE

Route 100, West Wardsboro, VT 05360. 802-896-8491. *Innkeepers*: Bobbe and Ray Price. Open all year.

Located only five miles from Mount Snow, the Green Mountain House has been a popular stopping place for visitors to this area since 1825. The original tavern was actually constructed in 1790 and improvements have been made continually. The Prices are both active in YMCA work and have geared their inn to groups of young people such as the Women's National Cross-Country Ski Team as well as to families and other guests. Originally a popular summer rest stop, the recent explosion of interest in winter sports has made the inn a year-round operation. Cross-country skiing is available on the premises. The Prices like to think of their inn as a home away from home with cheery fires and home-cooked food (for guests only). *Room Rates*: $12 to $26 per person, MAP. Larger groups of 40 or more may book well in advance for special group rates. Pets are permitted. *Driving Instructions*: The inn is located on Route 100. It is about five miles north of the *Mount Snow Ski Area*.

Weston, Vermont

Weston is a tiny Vermont town (population 500) with a small village green. It has several tourist attractions, including the *Farrar-Mansur House*, with its collection of local antiques housed in a restored tavern; the *Vermont Guild Craftsmen*, which is both a museum of old tools and an outlet for contemporary crafts; and the *Vermont Country Store*, one of the state's finest old-time stores. During the summer the *Weston Playhouse* presents a full season of summer theater. The *Weston Bowl Mill* is open daily to the public with tours of bowl and other woodenware manufacturing processes.

THE INN AT WESTON

Route 100, Box 56, Weston, VT 05161. 802-824-5804. *Innkeepers*: Sue and Stu Douglas. Open June 15 to Oct. 31, Nov. 15 to Apr. 1.

The Inn at Weston was described by one visitor as "the friendliest place in New England" and it may well be that. The young innkeepers, Stu and Sue Douglas, have taken an old Vermont farm which was originally a cheese factory and created a homey, inviting inn with a wonderful restaurant featuring home cooking. Built in 1848, the inn has 13 guest rooms, 7 with private baths. Some of the guest rooms are in the recently converted hayloft. Children are welcome here and there is a game room complete with television for their entertainment. The inn has its original wide board floors and the dining room is paneled with old barn board. Guests can select from a menu that changes daily and reflects Mrs. Douglas' particular talent with both meat and vegetarian dishes (the latter require advance notice). All bread, piecrusts, and pastries are homemade, as are other desserts and soups. The menu reflects those ingredients that are fresh and in season. Typical selections include chilled poached salmon, $6.75; smoked loin of pork, $5.75; and Russian vegetable pie, $5. Prices are a la carte. *Room Rates*: In summer, double rooms, $22 to $25, including breakfast. In winter, $24 to $26 per person, MAP. No pets permitted. *Driving Instructions*: Take I-91 to exit 6, then take Route 103 north to Route 11 west. Follow Route 11 west to Route 100 north at Londonderry. Take Route 100 into Weston.

Wilmington, Vermont

Wilmington is located on scenic Route 100, sometimes known as the "Ski Highway." The village is near several ski areas including *Haystack* and *Hogback*. Also nearby is *Molly Stark State Park* with its camping, hiking, hunting, and fishing. For further area information, see also the area descriptions for Marlboro and West Dover.

THE HERMITAGE INN

Coldbrook Road, Wilmington, VT 05363. 802-464-3759. *Innkeeper*: Jim McGovern. Open all year.

The Hermitage has been developed from a farmhouse dating back to the 1700s. At one time it was the residence of Miss Bertha Eastman, who was the editor of the famed Social Register, the blue book of society. A number of years have passed since she made the farmhouse her home and the building and its grounds have since been extensively renovated by its present owner, Jim McGovern.

The reputation of the Hermitage rests primarily upon its cuisine. In fact, the restaurant is frequently recommended to visitors by other innkeepers. The inn has four separate intimate dining rooms. Among the specialties are an assortment of homemade soups, Wiener schnitzel, frogs legs Provençale, filet of sole Veronique, shrimps scampi, and chicken amandine. Daily specials often feature local game such as pheasant or quail. Desserts include items like Bananas Foster or peach Melba. The inn offers a complete Sunday brunch.

Each of the guest rooms at the Hermitage is individually deco-

rated and furnished with antiques. All have private baths and four have working fireplaces. The carriage house has a sauna.

Several years ago the Hermitage established a cross-country skiing center which has well-maintained marked trails laid out on the property's 100 acres. The inn offers equipment rentals and cross-country instruction; free shuttle to *Mount Snow* daily.

The Hermitage is a quiet, relaxing inn, free from the annoyance of television, radio, and telephones. It is a place to enjoy the comfortable rooms, excellent cuisine, and well-stocked wine cellar. *Room Rates*: Double rooms, $35; optional MAP available for $35 more a day for two people. *Driving Instructions* North on I-91 to the Brattleboro/Route 9 exit. Follow Route 9 to Wilmington. At the traffic light, go right onto Route 100. Go about three miles to Coldbrook Road on your left. The inn is another three miles down Coldbrook Road.

Woodstock, Vermont (including South Woodstock)

Woodstock is one of Vermont's most popular towns, with its old homes and shops and oval village green. It has been a favorite summer residence for artists, authors, musicians, and teachers for years. There is excellent golf and tennis available at the *Woodstock Country Club* (their golf course was designed by Robert Trent Jones) as well as horseback riding at the *Green Mountain Horse Association* with its miles of forest trails. The village of Woodstock operates a recreation center with facilities for bowling, billiards, swimming, basketball, and skating, plus community tennis courts and a hockey rink. Sports' lovers enjoy excellent upland bird shooting, deer hunting, and trout fishing in the local brooks, rivers, and lakes. Tourists who are fond of local history will enjoy the *Dana House* operated by the Woodstock Historical Society and *Perkins Academy* in South Woodstock. South Woodstock is also home of the Doscher Country School of Photography, a summer photography workshop in operation for more than 30 years.

KEDRON VALLEY INN

Route 106, South Woodstock, VT 05071. 802-457-1473. Mailing Address: Box 145, South Woodstock, VT 05071. *Innkeepers*: Paul and Barbara Kendall. Open all year.

The Kedron Valley Inn has numerous activities for all members of the family right on the property. It maintains an excellent riding stable with horses and instruction available to guests. The inn also offers guests sleigh or wagon rides. In addition, the Green Mountain Horse Association, adjacent to the inn, has laid out numerous riding trails through the woods. The Kedron Valley also has a nice "swimming hole" which offers, additionally, summer fishing and winter skating (lighted at night). Cross-country skiers are drawn to the inn not only for its own popular trails but for those of the *Woodstock Touring Center*. There is also a paddle tennis court, so enthusiasts should bring along their paddles.

The Kedron Valley Inn has 34 guest rooms, all but four with private baths. The inn offers typical Vermont country inn rooms within the original early nineteenth-century building, as well as eight modern motel-type rooms in a recently constructed log-cabin style building. Two of the inn's rooms have fireplaces and two have parlor stoves. In addition, there are fireplaces in the living room, lobby, dining room, and lounge.

Meals at the inn are open to guests and the public and generally consist of simple, country-style cooking, with entrees such as omelets, baked stuffed shrimp, maple-cured ham, and home-baked breads and desserts. There is a special Sunday brunch with a large selection of items including eggs Benedict, blueberry pancakes, and quiche Lorraine. Dinner prices range from $7 to $9 complete (some special appetizers or desserts bring the total higher). The complete brunches range from $3.75 to $8.50 with appetizers and alcoholic beverages additional. *Room Rates*: Double rooms, $7 to $18 per person. Single rooms and rooms in the motel unit are higher. A service charge is added to bills for meals (not for rooms) in lieu of tipping. Pets are permitted. *Driving Instructions*: The inn is five miles south of Woodstock on Route 106. Woodstock can be reached from Rt. I-89 (exit 1, west to Woodstock) or I-91 (exit 8, left on Rt. 131, 8 miles then right on Rt. 106, 12 miles).

NORTHERN

Bradford, Vermont

Bradford is a small farming community of 2000 persons located in the Connecticut River Valley not too far from Hanover, NH. Bradford is the scene of an annual *November Wild Game Supper* which has attracted some national attention. There are numerous country fairs held in the area during the warmer months. Golf, tennis, boating, and canoeing are all available in Bradford. Glider trips are available at the airport in Post Mills, about 10 miles away. Downhill skiing is across the river at the *Dartmouth Skiway* in Lyme, NH.

MERRY MEADOW FARM

Lower Plain, Bradford, VT 05033. 802-222-4412. *Innkeeper*: Mrs. Betty M. Williams. Open to guests all year except for July and August, when it is a riding school and summer camp for children.

The Merry Meadow Farm is a working horse farm in the Connecticut River Valley consisting of a 14-room farmhouse with attached and separate barns and a number of riding rings. The farmhouse has three modern baths and a huge kitchen with a beamed ceiling and a wood-burning stove. Guests are welcome to participate in daily farm activities such as feeding the animals, gathering berries, bringing in wood, mending fences, or hitching a pony to a cart. In the winter there is cross-country skiing on the premises and downhill skiing nearby. Special care is taken to ensure that children will be able to enjoy all the facets of farm life. Meals are home-cooked, of course, and served family style in the sunny farmhouse kitchen. Some of the favorite dishes include stuffed cabbage, beef Stroganoff, fried chicken, and homemade pies and pastries. Much

of the produce served comes from the farm garden or the berry patch. *Room Rates*: Adults, $25 per person and children $18 per person, AP. This includes riding privileges, but not lessons. Pets are permitted. *Driving Instructions*: Take exit 16 off I-91 to Route 5 south. Then take Route 5 south 4¼ miles; the farmhouse and stables are on the right. (Look for sign in front of house.)

Brookfield, Vermont

In 1813 a person walking across the frozen pond at Brookfield drowned when he broke through the thin ice. This prompted the village to build, in 1819–20, the first of a series of floating bridges made of wood over barrels. The latest of these was built in 1936 and is still in daily use. This bridge and the adjoining pond form the focus of this scenic village that was recently placed on the list of designated Vermont Historic Districts, just in time to save the bridge from being paved over. At one time as many as 20 mills obtained their power from a short stretch of the local brook and pond. Most of these exist today only as abandoned foundations. Nearby *Allis State Park* has camping and picnicking facilities, as well as an observation tower.

GREEN TRAILS COUNTRY INN

By the Floating Bridge, Brookfield, VT 05036. 802-276-2012. *Innkeepers*: the Williams and Taylor families. Open from December through March and from May through October.

The Green Trails Country Inn is a complex of buildings put up between 1790 and 1850. It includes the inn itself with its six guest rooms and a country store, a restored Fork Shop (pitchfork and rake manufacturing place) which is now a restaurant, a riding stable, and the residences occupied by the two families who restored the buildings and now run all activities there. The inn itself has rooms furnished in Victorian and early American style. In addition to these old-fashioned inn rooms, there are four efficiency apartments located in adjoining buildings for guests who wish to live more independently during their stay. Green Trails is located near a floating bridge erected by the village in 1819–20. Many winter guests use the inn as a base for enjoying the excellent cross-country skiing trails that originate there, as well as the downhill areas in central Vermont. Cross-country skiing instruction is available on weekends; at other times lessons can be arranged by appointment. Summer visitors may swim in Sunset Lake, relax at the private beach owned by the inn, and also enjoy hiking, fishing, and picnicking. Horseback riding is available at the *Green Trails Stables.*

Dining in the Forks Restaurant is open to the public and features a small, interesting menu with a la carte selections such as lobster pie ($5.95), chicken Kiev ($5.50), and Wiener schnitzel ($4.95). The restaurant is decorated with antique forks, rakes, and tools and has a working player piano. *Room Rates*: Double room with private bath, $24. The efficiency apartments range from $40 to $60 per night. No pets permitted. *Driving Instructions*: Bear right at the fork on Route 66; follow to Route 14 north for six miles to East Brookfield. Follow sign to Floating Bridge and Green Trails (two miles up the Brookfield State Highway from Route 14).

Craftsbury Common, Vermont

Craftsbury Common, with its hilltop views of the accompanying countryside, its mountainous backdrops, and its many country gardens is certainly one of Vermont's most extraordinary sights. This village is most inviting to tourists every season of the year. There is hiking and canoeing in the summer and wonderful cross-country skiing in the winter. The village is 25 miles from Stowe so it can provide a place to stay for those who wish to ski there but avoid the bustle of that famous area. Craftsbury Common is an absolute gem in the countryside, which has remained unchanged for over 100 years and yet is in no way primitive.

THE INN ON THE COMMON

Main Street, Craftsbury Common, VT 05827. 802-586-9619.
Innkeepers: Penny and Michael Schmitt.

The Inn on the Common consists of two restored Federal buildings (originally a private house and a cabinet and sleigh shop, respectively) which currently are filled with a mixture of antiques and contemporary furniture. The Schmidts take great pride in their antiques, many of which are heirlooms, and in the extensive art work on the walls. The grounds have an English croquet court, clay tennis court, bocce court, swimming pool, and some of the area's most attractive gardens. Several of the 11 guest rooms have working fireplaces and/or bathrooms with skylights. All rooms share bath facilities. The innkeepers also own a farm in neighboring Greensboro which guests may wish to explore.

Dining is a special occasion at the inn. Children eat at an earlier hour so that adults may enjoy their dinners without interruption. Whenever possible, meals feature vegetables and herbs grown on the inn grounds.

The inn has its own craft shop, free of gimmickry, called the "Common Market." Winter visitors can enjoy cross-country skiing at the inn or on nearby trails. Ski instruction is available. The inn can arrange for outings in the local countryside in any season. *Room Rates*: Double rooms, $32 to $37 per person, MAP. Bed and breakfast rates are from $20 to $25 per person, with single room

rates higher. Other plans, including a two-room suite, are available. A 15 percent gratuity charge and applicable taxes are added to the bill. Reservations are a necessity. Pets are permitted if special arrangements are made in advance. *Driving Instructions*: Take Route 14 from the Montpelier-Barre area north to the village of Craftsbury Common.

East Burke, Vermont

East Burke is in the heart of what Senator George Aiken called the "Northeast Kingdom"—the three Vermont counties of Essex, Orleans, and Caldonia. Located about 15 miles north of St. Johnsbury and about 35 miles south of the Canadian border, this small farming community is noted for its *Burke Mountain Ski Area* and the *Darling State Park*. The park has facilities for picnicking, hiking, trout fishing, and hunting, as well as nature trails. The downhill ski area has 3 slopes and 23 trails served by a double chair lift, two Poma lifts, and a T-bar. Snow-making machinery is available.

Nearby St. Johnsbury is the home of the *Maple Grove Museum*, located at the world's largest maple candy factory.

DARION INN AT BURKLYN

Darling Hill Road, East Burke, VT 05832. 802-626-9332. Mailing Address: Box 12, East Burke, VT 05832. *Innkeeper*: Gordon Watkins; owner: Marshall Thurber. Open all year.

Elmer Darling was a Vermonter who once owned the old Fifth Avenue Hotel in New York City. In 1908 he retired and was drawn back to his native state, where, in its "Northeast Kingdom," he used his considerable resources to build the renowned Burklyn estate. Adjacent to the area's spectacular Mountainview Farm, the estate was centered around a 35-room mansion high on a ridge. While Mr. Darling was alive, the estate included the 750-acre farm and all its facilities. After his death, the mansion was sold separately but the recent purchase of both pieces of property by Marshall Thurber has reunited them.

The Burklyn mansion is currently being restored and will become a conference center in the near future. In the meantime the original farmhouse for Mountainview, built in 1880 and renovated in 1969, serves as the Darion Inn. Set in an area of rolling hills, pastures, and views of nearby Burke Mountain, the inn offers 19 guest rooms with private or connecting baths, a restaurant in the converted Darling creamery building, and a fully equipped equestrian center housed in the large red barns that are part of the farm. The riding facilities include stables with 38 horses and a 15,000 square-foot indoor riding arena. The inn also has a Ski Touring Center which includes a complete ski shop and 25 miles of marked, groomed trails. In addition to the guest room facilities, there is a bunk room for skiers who prefer a more informal setting.

The decor here is simple and the atmosphere is warm and inviting. The 750 acres surrounding the farm and estate give the inn a kind of built-in seclusion. Meals are served from a limited menu that changes daily and includes a single chef's special, steak, and a vegetarian dish. *Room Rates*: Double rooms, $30; single rooms are less. Family suites with two bedrooms and a connecting bath are $46. Add $11 per person for MAP. There are also five-day special rates. Pets are permitted in the inn kennel only; baby-sitting service is available. *Driving Instructions*: From St. Johnsbury, take I-91 north to exit 23. Follow Route 5 north through Lyndonville to Route 114. Bear right on 114 and follow for five miles to East Burke. There, turn left just after the Exxon station. Keep left, up the hill one mile to the inn.

Greensboro, Vermont

Greensboro is a small community in northeastern Vermont most noted for Caspian Lake, a fine fishing and water sports area. The neighboring town of Craftsbury has a number of interesting attractions (see Craftsbury Common).

HIGHLAND LODGE

Craftsbury Road, Greensboro, VT 05841. 802-533-2647. *Innkeepers*: Carol and Dave Smith. Open from Memorial Day weekend to October 15 and from December 22 to April 1.

The Highland is a wide, two-story lake-front inn with a full-length porch. Most of the inn dates from 1926, although one part was a farmhouse for a sheep farm prior to that. Ten nonhousekeeping cottages have been added over the years to the 180-acre property bordering Caspian Lake. The lodge provides a number of activities for guests, including cookouts, swimming in the lake, boating, canoeing, sailing, paddle boating, badminton, and croquet. There is good lake fishing for salmon, lake trout, rainbow trout, and perch. In the winter the lodge offers daily instruction in cross-country skiing as well as equipment rentals and sales in the ski shop and guided or self-guided tours along their marked trails. The lodge is decorated with some antiques and a variety of sturdy colonial-style furniture from local Vermont furniture manufacturers.

At dinner the menu offers entrees such as top sirloin of beef,

roast turkey, fish filet with shrimp sauce, roast leg of lamb, coq au vin, Burgundy beef, and baked pork loin, among others. *Room Rates*: In the lodge, $47.50 to $65 including gratuities for two persons, MAP. Cottage rates vary according to occupancy and season. No pets permitted. *Driving Instructions*: Take Route 15 to Route 16 (east of Hardwick) where you turn north. Take Route 16 to East Hardwick and follow the signs to Caspian Lake.

Lincoln, Vermont

Lincoln is located on the famed hiking *Long Trail* adjacent to the Green Mountain National Forest in central Vermont, northeast of Middlebury. The New Haven River with its lovely waterfalls passes through the village. Nearby Middlebury offers more formal tourist attractions.

THE LONG RUN

Lincoln Gap Road, Lincoln Center, VT Mailing Address: RFD #1, Box 114, Bristol VT 05443. 802-453-3233. *Innkeeper*: Gen and Jim Burke. Open all year except in November and April.

The Long Run is a lovely, gabled village inn in the mountain town of Lincoln. Overlooking the New Haven River, the inn was a lumberjack hotel in the 1800s. Constructed in 1799 and expanded later to twenty rooms, the inn has two dining rooms, a fireplace lounge, and a large "rocking chair" porch. It is part of an inn-to-inn cross-country skiing package (see the Tulip Tree Inn in Chittenden) during the winter and a similar "Hike Inn-to-Inn" package in the summer (average daily per person charges for the packages are $25 plus lunch).

The inn is a popular place for enjoying cross-country skiing in the winter and swimming (water hole in the river in front of the inn), hiking (the famous Long Train is nearby), and bicycling in the summer months. Horseback riding trips that go inn to inn also stop here. For details, write the inn or to Country Roads Horse Trekking, Box 16, Middlebury, VT 05753.

The Long Run serves simple, country meals with homemade bread, cakes, soups, garden salads in season, beef Burgundy, and roast turkey among the items served. Apple pancakes with maple syrup, sausage, and bacon is a special favorite at the inn. *Room Rates*: Six guest rooms share three baths approximately $20 per person, MAP. *Driving Instructions*: Take Route 7 north of Middlebury then to Route 17. Take Route 17 east to Bristol. In Bristol, turn right at the second stone bridge outside the village (Lincoln Gap Road). Go five miles to Lincoln Center and the inn.

Lower Waterford, Vermont

Lower Waterford, the center of the maple syrup industry, is one of the most photographed and painted villages in Vermont. The white houses of the village look across the Connecticut River to a marvelous view of the White Mountains in the distance. Route 18 crosses the river here and provides the traveler with access to the New Hampshire mountains via Littleton, NH. Nearby St. Johnsbury is a larger Vermont town with a population of approximately 8500 and a number of interesting tourist attractions. These include the *Fairbanks Museum of Natural History* which has a wide-ranging collection of exhibits on magnetism, light and electricity, botany, plant life, birds, tools, and technology. The *St. Johnsbury Athenaeum* has a collection of Hudson River School paintings and sculpture. There is also a *Maple Museum* with syrup production in season, a year-round exhibit about the industry, and tours of the maple sugar factory.

THE RABBIT HILL INN

Pucker Street, Lower Waterford, VT 05848. 802-748-9766. *Innkeepers*: Nancy and Ed Ludwig. Open all year.

The four, large hand-hewn Doric columns that support the front porch of the Rabbit Hill give it a somewhat imposing look that certainly belies its relaxed atmosphere. The property consists of a main inn built around the year 1825 and enlarged about 15 years later to its present size. It has always served as an inn except for a short period when it was used as a private home. In its early days, the inn served the active logging community in the area and the floors still bear the marks of the spiked boots of the drovers and lumberjacks who stopped there. The "Briar Patch," a smaller building put up in 1795, currently houses a gift shop below and

some old-fashioned guest rooms above. In the mid-1850s a third building was constructed consisting of a ballroom with a carriage house and woodsheds below. The ballroom has been subdivided into a number of motel-type rooms.

Guests who stay in this inviting inn can choose their accommodations according to their preference for more contemporary or old-fashioned surroundings. All rooms have private baths and five have working fireplaces. Fireplaces and Franklin stoves are also found in the common room. For the guests' enjoyment there is cross-country skiing on the property, spectacular views of New Hampshire's White Mountains, and a large nearby lake for swimming, boating, and fishing.

Two connecting dining rooms serve an interesting variety of seafood, meat, and poultry dishes with names like Barre Pike Beefsteak, Vermont Drovers Journey End Steak, Veal Waterford, and Breast of Chicken Burlington. A complete dinner of appetizer, soup, entree, and dessert, served with "cheese tasty, relish tray, salad, potato, vegetable, and hot, homemade bread" should average $9 to $11. Children's plates are available. The inn serves breakfast and dinner to both guests and the public and will prepare box lunches for guests upon request. *Room Rates*: Double occupancy, $22 for motel-type rooms in the 1855 Annex; $24 for inn rooms without fireplace, $28 with fireplace; $30 for two doubles with fireplace; $34 for a two-room suite with connecting bath and fireplace. There are deductions for singles and additions for extra people in the rooms. Pets are permitted. *Driving Instructions*: Route 91 north to Route 2, then west to Route 18, and south for seven miles to inn. Or Route 93 north to Route 18 in Littleton, NH, then seven miles north to inn.

Middlebury, Vermont

Middlebury is best known, of course, for Middlebury College and its lovely New England campus. However, the town of 7,000 is more than a college town. One of its most important attractions is the *State Craft Center at Frog Hollow*, where hundreds of Vermont artisans (on a rotating basis) have workshops, display galleries, and salesrooms. The town has many fine antique shops, and *Van Raalte* has an outlet store there with low prices on men's and women's clothing. Skiers can enjoy both alpine and cross-country skiing at the *Middlebury College Snow Bowl*, which is about 10 miles outside of town. There is further cross-country skiing at the college itself. Summer visitors enjoy boating and sailing on *Lake Dunmore* and golf at the *Middlebury College Golf Course. The Sheldon Museum* and the *Morgan Horse Farm* are open during the warmer months. Middlebury College sponsors a winter carnival in February, and there are two county fairs nearby in the summer: the *Bristol County Agricultural Fair* and the *Addison County Farm and Field Days*.

MIDDLEBURY INN AND MOTEL

17 Pleasant Street, Middlebury, VT 05753. Mailing Address: Box 631, Middlebury, VT 05753. 802-388-4961. *Innkeeper*: Frank T. Emmanuel. Open all year.

The Middlebury Inn, overlooking the village green, consists of a large red brick building first constructed in 1827, a brick annex, and a recently constructed 20-unit motel building. It is a fine example of a dignified town inn with a special tone set by the nearby college. The rooms are somewhat old-fashioned and homey in the 1827 building, while the annex and motel units are more modern. The dining room serves country-style meals including

maple-cured ham, but the current innkeepers are planning to completely redo the menu early in 1978. *Room Rates*: In the inn, single rooms, $14; double rooms, $26 to $34; a two-room suite with connecting bath, $46. Rooms in the inn with shared bath are less. Motel units have rooms from $32 to $36. *Driving Instructions*: From Boston, take I-93 to I-89, then Route 4 to Route 7. From Albany take the Northway to exit 20, then take Route 149 to Route 4 to Route 22A to Route 73 to Route 30.

Milton, Vermont

Milton is located north of Burlington and adjacent to *Arrowhead Mountain Lake*. The village is about five miles from the *Sand Bar Wildlife Area* and a short drive from the Champlain Islands including South Hero, Grand Isle, North Hero, the Alburgs, and Isle La Motte. Recreational opportunities include trail riding; fishing, swimming, and boating in Lake Champlain; and weekly auctions during the summer months in Milton. There are also the attractions of Burlington and the *Shelburne Museum* to the south.

MAYVILLE ACRES FARM

RFD 2, Milton, VT 05468. 802-893-2273. *Innkeepers*: C. Edward and Elaine Mayville. Open from June through October.

Vacationers wishing to spend a week or more on a working farm in northern Vermont will enjoy a stay at the Mayville Acres Farm, with its big porches and huge willow trees in front. Indeed, guests have come from as far away as Israel, Australia, and England to stay with the Mayvilles. This is a working dairy farm where guests are allowed to participate in all aspects of farm life. Housekeeping accommodations, with private bath, are in the large farmhouse. *Room Rates*: $100 per week, per family. Drive east on Main St., take left at crossroads, and stop at second farm on right.

THE WRIGHT PLACE

Westford Road, Milton, VT 05468. 802-893-4900. *Innkeepers*: Patrick and Lori Wright. Open all year.

The Wright Place is not an old country inn; rather it is a new, three-story log cabin surrounded by a small farm complete with farm animals. It offers to guests the warm, family atmosphere of a farm vacation along with the conveniences made possible by contemporary construction. The farm provides a variety of recreational activities for all ages. For children, there are pony rides, a sandbox, sledding and skating in winter, a brook for wading in summer, and, when needed, a baby-sitter. For adults, there are horses and trails, cross-country skiing, fishing or ice fishing.

The lodge is small and accommodates guests in only four rooms which share a bath. Meals are served to guests only and feature dinners with home-raised, country-cured ham, Yankee pot roast, chili soup, hot muffins and breads, pies, cakes, and jams. *Room*

Rates: Adults, $19 per day or $90 per week; children, $11 per day or $30 to $60 per week, AP. Riding is included. Babies free. No pets permitted. *Driving Instructions*: Take Route 7 to the blinking light in Milton and turn east. The lodge is 1⅓ miles on the right.

North Hero, Vermont (the Champlain Islands)

This area was originally very sparsely settled because of its inaccessibility in the middle of Lake Champlain. However, the area gained some prominence when 64-acre lots were deeded to Ethan Allen and the Green Mountain Boys as rewards for services performed in the defense of their country during the Revolution. Now the Champlain Islands are mostly summer colonies and serve as logical stopping points for the exploration of the Lake Champlain-Burlington area. In nearby South Hero is the *Hyde Log Cabin*, thought to be the oldest log cabin in the country.

NORTH HERO HOUSE

North Hero, VT 05474. 802-372-8237. *Innkeepers*: Roger and Caroline Sorg. Open from late June through Labor Day.

The North Hero House is actually a complex of buildings dating from the 1800s. The main inn is a three-story house built in 1890. Additional accommodations are available in fully restored lake-side

homesteads and a restored country store. The waterfront area provides excellent swimming as well as a carefully preserved steamship dock. Rooms are decorated with sturdy contemporary country-style furniture and attractive wallpaper or paneling on the walls. Motor boating, canoeing, sailing, swimming, and fishing for bass, walleye, and northern pike are among the many activities available to guests at the North Hero House. The dining room serves abundant meals from a different menu every evening. It is open to the public, space permitting. *Room Rates*: Single rooms, $14 to $28; double rooms, $16 to $28. Most rooms have private baths (except for 2 of the 22 guest rooms). No pets permitted. *Driving Instructions*: From Burlington, go north on I-89 to exit 17 and then north on Island Route 2 to North Hero. From the N.Y. Thruway (Northway) take exit 39 at Plattsburg and follow signs to the "Ferry to Vermont." Upon leaving the ferry, turn left onto Route 2. Then turn left off Route 2 and proceed to the inn.

Rochester, Vermont

Rochester is located in central Vermont, north of Rutland, in the heart of the *Green Mountain National Forest*. Located nearby are several state recreation areas, including the *Texas Falls*, *Chitten Brook*, *Brandon Brook*, and *Robert Frost* recreational areas. The *Middlebury College Snow Bowl* is only 20 minutes from Rochester.

HARVEY'S MOUNTAIN VIEW LODGE AND FARM

Rochester, VT 05767. 802-767-8783. *Innkeepers*: Donald and Madeline Harvey. Open all year.

Harvey's is an 1810 white-shingled farmhouse to which a much more recent addition has been made. This is a working farm with barns and animals. It has seven guest rooms with semiprivate baths. Among the activities available to guests are a swimming pool, fishing in either of two ponds, a pony for children to ride, and two horses that can be used by older guests. The farm also offers relaxation, leisurely strolls through the pastures, and, perhaps, a visit to the barns at milking time. Home-cooked, farm-style meals are served and guests may bring their own wine. Some of the surrounding farmland is being developed as vacation and re-

tirement home sites by the Harveys and guests are invited to visit the development area. *Room Rates*: Adults, $18 per person, MAP; children $3 less. No children under four years of age and no pets permitted. *Driving Instructions*: Three miles off Route 100 in Rochester, VT. East up the hill from the village green.

The Valley, Vermont

The Valley is the area surrounding the four north central villages of Waitsfield, Fayston, Moretown, and Warren. The Valley itself is surrounded by three of Vermont's more famous ski areas—*Glen Ellen, Mad River, and Sugarbush*. It is an area of both rolling hillside farmland and breathtaking mountains. Sugarbush, located in the village of Warren, is a superb ski area with a gondola tramway and six other ski lifts. On Columbus Day weekend Sugarbush holds an *Oktoberfest* with a flea market and a sidewalk art sale. Sugarbush also has indoor tennis, pools, saunas, movies, skating, and ski touring. Summer activities include golf and tennis tournaments and soaring meets. Warren also is known for its Fourth of July celebration. Waitsfield is the home of the Glen Ellen and Mad River ski areas with five and four lifts, respectively. The *Bundy Art Gallery* in Waitsfield has collections of contemporary painting and sculpture. The village is filled with antique and crafts shops and also has a covered bridge. The abundance of skiers in the winter has brought a myriad of contemporary and traditional restaurants to this region featuring almost all international cuisines as well as traditional Vermont country cooking.

Waitsfield (see The Valley, Vermont)

MILLBROOK LODGE

RFD Box 44, Waitsfield, VT 05673. 802-496-2405. *Innkeepers*: Bill and Mary Stewart. Open all year.

The Millbrook Lodge is a renovated 1847 farmhouse with six guest rooms. The Stewarts cater to young people and families in a friendly, informal atmosphere. The inn, furnished with antiques, has a comfortable living room with a fireplace and a sitting room with an antique Glenwood parlor stove. The Stewarts serve country-style meals, including fresh-baked breads, pie, and cakes, to their guests only. *Room Rates*: From $9 per person for a bunk room with no meals to $21 for a family room with private bath, MAP. All rates are subject to Vermont 5 percent tax and a 10 percent service charge. Some "well behaved outside pets" are allowed. *Driving Instructions*: Take Route 100 to Waitsfield and then Route 17 west ⅛ mile to the inn.

KNOLL FARM COUNTRY INN

Bragg Hill Road, RFD, Waitsfield, VT 05673. 802-496-3939. *Innkeepers*: Ann Day Heinzerling and Bill Heinzerling. Open all year except in April and November.

The Knoll Farm Inn, on 150 acres of hillside pasture and woods, is a converted farmhouse with five guest rooms, a huge family kitchen, dining room, study, and living room. The farm has a red barn and a smaller barn/shop. The barn is used to hold the 30 tons of hay needed to maintain the farm's 20 animals. This was a working farm in the 1800s and was converted to a combination farm and inn in 1937. The farm continues to produce its own meats, vegetables, eggs, fruits, milk, butter, and breads. Dinners feature these ingredients in hearty meals, including pot roasts, pork roasts, tomato puddings, sausage, jellies and jams. The Heinzerlings serve

what may be the biggest breakfast in any Vermont inn, using their own fresh ingredients and featuring blueberry pancakes on Sunday mornings.

The inn has its own pond with a dock and a rowboat. There is good skating here in the winter. Mrs. Heinzerling is an accomplished naturalist known in the area for her nature talks and slide shows; she is happy to guide the inn's guests on various nature walks. Riding horses and horsemanship clinics are available. The inn has a collection of old buggies and sleighs which are used for rides. Guests are welcome to help with any chores from milking to mending fences, but they are not made to feel obliged to help. For those who wish, there is tennis, golf, white-water canoeing, polo, and rugby, all nearby. Vermont's Long Trail is only four miles away. *Room Rates*: Adults, $19 per person in double rooms which share hall baths; children under 13, $12 per person, MAP. Weekly rates are also available. Children under three years old and pets are not permitted. *Driving Instructions*: The farm is ½ mile up the hill (Bragg Hill Road) from the junction of Routes 100 and 17.

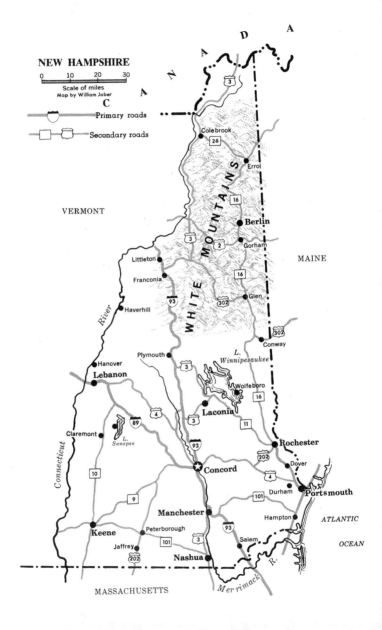

NEW HAMPSHIRE

Scale of miles
Map by William Jaber

Primary roads
Secondary roads

New Hampshire

In 1623, following several earlier exploratory parties, Samuel Thomson and his followers formed the first permanent white settlement in the future state at what is now Dover, New Hampshire. Early grants for the property of the state were given to a Captain John Mason in 1629. The earliest real property settlements were in the Portsmouth area, because the harsh weather of the inland sections, as well as continuing difficulties with the Indian tribes, made living and travel there difficult.

In its infancy, New Hampshire was first part of Massachusetts, later a royal province of England, and finally part of Massachusetts again, in time to join the growing feeling of discontent with the colonial rule of England. During the Revolution, one of New Hampshire's military leaders, General John Stark, joined his forces with those of the Green Mountain Boys to meet the advancing British troops of General Burgoyne and rout them in a decisive battle outside Bennington, Vermont. This battle was the turning point for Burgoyne, who finally surrendered at Saratoga.

Today, New Hampshire is not only famous for tourism but for thriving industrial communities as well. It is generally divided into six major centers for tourism. These include the Seacoast Region, around Portsmouth; the White Mountain Region, the area of the tallest mountains in the east; the Lakes Region with the great Lake Winnipesaukee as well as Squam Lake, Lake Winnisquam, and many smaller lakes; the Dartmouth–Lake Sunapee Region to the west of the Winnipesaukee area; the Monadnock Region, named for its famous mountain; and the Merrimack Valley Region, which includes the Merrimack River and the three largest cities in the state—Concord, Manchester, and Nashua.

Vacationers can get help in planning their trip to this state by writing to the State Division of Economic Development, State House Annex, Box 856, Concord, NH 03301. The telephone number is 603-271-2666.

SOUTHERN

Bradford (see Dartmouth–Lake Sunapee Region)

THE BRADFORD INN
Main Street, Bradford, NH 03221. 603-938-5309. *Innkeepers*: Thomas C. and Ethel M. Best. Open all year.

There has been an inn at the Bradford's Main Street location for 200 years, although the Bradford Inn dates from the early 1890s. The Bests bought the old Bradford Hotel in 1976 and have been gradually remaking it into a true country inn, with 12 guest rooms, only 1 with a private bath. It is decorated with antiques gathered over the years.

The Bests' describe their inn as a "place for rustic romantics who relish the casual luxury of sleeping in country comfort, dining on home-cooked specialties and reaping the daily rewards of New England life." Meals are prepared by Mr. Best, who offers dinner guests a selection of six basic entrees including boneless chicken breast, beef in wine, ham steak, lobster Newburg, and two types of steak. Dinner prices range from $6 to $9.50, a la carte. *Room*

Rates: From $14. *Driving Instructions*: The inn is located near the junction of Routes 114 and 103.

The Dartmouth–Lake Sunapee Region (including Bradford, Canaan, Georges Mills, Hanover, Lyme, New London, Newbury, Sunapee, and Webster, New Hampshire)

The Lake Sunapee area is rich in history as well as its more easily recognized recreational opportunities. The area includes Dartmouth College, in Hanover, *Old Fort No. 4* (a replica of an old stockade) in Charlestown, *Webster Meeting House Museum* in Webster, and the *Saint Gaudens National Historic Site* in Cornish, among other attractions. There are eight state parks and recreational areas within the confines of these towns, including *Mount Sunapee State Park* with its spacious beach and enclosed gondola ride to the top of a 2700-foot peak. Almost every recreation available in the state is here with the exception of a major downhill skiing center. Golf is available at the area's nine golf courses, and swimming is possible at hundreds of locations. In addition, there is boating, fishing, hunting, hiking, horseback riding, tennis, and picnicking. Numerous country fairs are held each summer and fall, and country auctions and antique hunting along back roads offer pleasant pastimes. Theater lovers enjoy year-round theater at the *Hopkins Center* at Dartmouth and the summer theater presented by the New London Players in that town.

East Hebron, New Hampshire

East Hebron is located on the shores of Newfound Lake a few miles south of Plymouth, NH, and a short drive from the White Mountain National Forest. *Wellington State Park*, across the lake from East Hebron, has swimming at one of the state's finest inland beaches, facilities for picnicking, and hiking. It is a short drive to the *Polar Caves* in Plymouth, where there are tours of the glacial caves as well as a maple sugar house, a waterfowl exhibit, and a nature trail.

HILLSIDE INN

Route 3A, Newfound Lake, East Hebron, NH 03232. 603-744-2413. *Innkeeper*: Fitzmaurice Kelley. Open almost all year.

The Hillside is a huge, rambling inn with porches, decks, and gables jutting out in a most interesting manner. The inn has evolved slowly from its first building, which was constructed in 1760, until the latest, finished in 1972. The result is a typical New Hampshire lake-front inn with accessory buildings nearby. The place combines the feeling of an antique-filled country inn with some of the pleasures of a small resort. Among the latter are the tennis courts, the beach, the game room, shuffleboard, croquet, and Ping-Pong. The main inn features four separate living rooms that are filled with antiques, two grand pianos, and four fireplaces. In addition, there are large cottages that have two or three bedrooms, tub and shower, and fireplaces in their living rooms. These cottages do not have housekeeping facilities and are, with one exception, closed during the winter months.

The inn serves both breakfast and dinner to guests and the public. The dinner menu features veal, steak, and roast beef. Recreational activities include swimming, sailing, fishing, and tennis in the warmer months and skiing at several nearby areas in the winter. *Room Rates*: From July through October, $17.50 to $20 per person, double occupancy, AP. Off season, $12.50 to $15 per person. No pets permitted except in the family cottages. *Driving Instructions*: North on I-93 to exit 23, then seven miles west on Route 104 to Bristol. North on 3A eight miles to the inn.

Fitzwilliam (see the Monadnock Region)

FITZWILLIAM INN

Route 119, Fitzwilliam, NH 03447. 603-585-9000. *Innkeepers*: Barbara and Charles Wallace. Open all year.

The Fitzwilliam Inn first opened its doors in 1796 and has continually provided lodging and food to travelers in the southwestern Monadnock Region. The inn is located at the end of the village green in a small, unspoiled village. There are 22 rooms, 7 with private baths. The pub is rustic, and the restaurant serves old-fashioned country-style food in the New England tradition. The inn has its own swimming pool for use in the summer, and many guests climb nearby Mount Monadnock. Winter visitors frequently ski at the nearby Fitzwilliam Ski Area or on several cross-country ski trails. *Room Rates*: Single rooms, $10 to $16; double rooms, $14 to $20. Pets are permitted. *Driving Instructions*: The inn is on the common just past the junction of Routes 12 and 119.

Henniker, New Hampshire

Henniker, founded in 1768, is a small New England village with a population of about 2200. It is the home of New England College, a private liberal arts school. The town is situated along the Contoocook River, with many lakes and ponds nearby. An old covered bridge crosses the river in Henniker. The town has many antique shops, and numerous auctions are held throughout the summer and fall.

The river and lakes provide fishing year-round as well as canoeing and swimming. Pat's Peak has excellent alpine skiing and the local Pole and Pedal Shop maintains 45 miles of marked cross-country trails. It's a short, scenic drive to Concord with its many summer theaters and state parks.

COLBY HILL INN

West Main Street, Henniker, NH 03242. 603-428-3281. *Innkeepers*: The Glover family. Open all year.

Colby Hill Inn is an attractive white country house, built around 1800. Once a working farm with five acres remaining, the many barns, sheds, and old stone walls offer a glimpse of the farm life of 100 years ago. The inn has eight spacious guest rooms, all comfortably furnished with antiques, four with private baths. Looking out the many-paned windows one is treated to open vistas of the surrounding hills and mountains. Guests can waken to the smell of freshly baked bread coming from the farm kitchen. The Glover's menu features traditional New England fare using locally produced

ingredients when available, including vegetables fresh from the farm garden. The inn serves breakfast to guests only, but is open to the public for dinner. Homemade soups and desserts are specialties of the house. There is a selection of wines, spirits, and lagers available with dinner.

Year-round and seasonal activities abound here, from canoeing and fly fishing in the many ponds and lakes in summer to white-water canoing and ice fishing in other seasons. And, of course, there is skiing—downhill at nearby areas plus 45 miles of local cross-country trails maintained by Pole and Pedal. *Room Rates*: Single rooms, $17 to $19; double rooms, $22 to $24; guest room with adjoining sitting room, $26. Children over six years old are welcome. Reservations are advised. No pets permitted. *Driving Instructions*: Take Henniker-Bradford exit off Routes 9 and 202. Take Route 114 south to town center. Turn right on Main Street about ½ mile to The Oaks. The inn is on the right, just off West Main.

Jaffrey (see the Monadnock Region)

WOODBOUND INN AND LAKE COTTAGES
Jaffrey, NH 03452. 603-532-8341. *Innkeepers*: The Brummer Family. Open from mid-May to mid-October and from December 26 to mid-March.

The Woodbound Inn and Cottages is a small resort on the lake front at Lake Contoocook. The resort is centered in a large white clapboard main building which dates, in part, from 1823. There are a number of pine-paneled cottages and a lodge annex that furnish additional housing for a total of 98 guests. The inn should appeal most to families and older visitors. On the grounds are a nine-hole golf course, a half-acre trout pond, and a tennis court as well as a ski slope with a rope tow and a barn where square dances are held. The inn rents both cross-country and downhill skiing equipment and offers instructions in both forms of skiing. Cross-country ski trails start at the inn. *Room Rates*: Rates are AP and include the use of all inn facilities. Rates for double rooms in the main building or lodge annex range from $25 for a room with shared bath to $32 for a room with fireplace and private bath. Cottages are about the same price with specific rentals depending on the number of people in the party. *Driving Instructions*: The inn is 2 miles from Routes 119 and 202 in southwest New Hampshire.

The Monadnock Region (including Antrim, Fitzwilliam, Hancock, Hillsboro, Jaffrey, Keene, Milford, Peterborough, Sharon, Troy, and Westmoreland, New Hampshire)

This is an active maple sugaring area with a good deal of industrial development in the immediate vicinity of Keene. This part of New Hampshire includes a number of family-style ski areas including *Crotched Mountain* and *Onset* outside of Bennington, Big Bear near the Massachusetts line in Brookline, NH, *Pinnacle Mountain* near East Sullivan, Temple Mountain outside of Peterborough, the *Fitzwilliam Ski Area* in Fitzwilliam, and *Pat's Peak* near Henniker.

Mount Monadnock, south of Troy, is one of the state's most popular visual and climbing peaks. There are a number of state parks in the confines of the Monadnock region including *Rhododendron State Park* near Mount Monadnock, *Miller State Park* near Peterborough, *Silver Lake State Park* south of Milford, *Greenfield State Park* in Greenfield, and *Monadnock State Park* outside Jaffrey.

Sightseeing might include a visit to the *Cathedral in the Pines* in Rindge, to the *Friendly Farm*, a farm of interest to children and others wishing to see farm animals up close and pet them; or to the *Old Fort No. 4* in Charlestown with its collection of seven fort buildings. The *Sharon Arts Center* on Route 123 has a large gallery and *Steamtown USA* has the world's largest collection of steam locomotives and equipment. This region, incidentally, has 7 covered bridges and more than 11 museums and historical buildings which are open to the public.

Northwood, New Hampshire

Northwood is a small town located about midway between Concord and Portsmouth and the same distance from the southernmost tip of Lake Winnipesaukee. The immediate area contains five lakes of some size—Jenness Pond, Northwood Lake, Bow Lake, Pleasant Pond, and Long Pond. The Blue Hills Range is nearby, with Catamount Mountain and Blue Job Mountain dominating the group. Two state parks are located here—*Bear Brook* and *Pawtuckaway*. *Rochester Country Club* has an eighteen-hole golf course.

THE RESORT AT LAKE SHORE FARM

Jenness Pond Road, Northwood, NH 03261. 603-942-5921, 942-5521. *Innkeepers*: Ellis and Eloise Ring. Open all year.

In April 1848, Reuben Watson wrote to his new wife HuldahJane "I hav ben to work upon our new house. I hav got the frame up. . . . I think you will like it." Thus began the construction of Lake Shore Farm. Today the farm, greatly enlarged, welcomes guests under the direction of members of the fifth generation of descendants of Reuben and HuldahJane.

Over the years the farmhouse grew and evolved with porches being added, closed in, and built over. In 1964 a modern annex was built near the main building to provide more rooms with private baths. Finally, a building was constructed to join the annex to the main house and provide more guest rooms and a large game room with fireplace and lounge. Recently constructed tennis courts add to the resort atmosphere. The inn is surrounded by sweeping lawns—once pastures—that slope gently toward Jenness Pond where there is a sandy beach for swimming. The inn also provides boats and canoes for relaxation or a try at fishing. Meals at the

farm are hearty country fare based on the abundance of fresh produce and dairy products that are available from the surrounding agricultural community. *Room Rates*: The inn operates on the American Plan, but 1978 rates were not available at the time of publication. *Driving Instructions*: Take Route 4 west of Concord past Route 28 to Route 107 north at Heritage Hardware. Follow Route 107 and turn off at the signs for Lake Shore Farm.

Plainfield (including Windsor, Vermont)

Plainfield is a small village near the Connecticut River south of Lebanon and Hanover. Because it is so near the famed Windsor Covered Bridge (the longest in Vermont) it is appropriate to include sightseeing activities in that area as well.

On the New Hampshire side of the river, the most important attraction in the immediate area is *Saint-Gaudens National Historic Site*. Augustus Saint-Gaudens (1848–1907) lived and worked here for several years and some of the buildings are open to the public.

Windsor was the birthplace of the Vermont constitution. *Constitution House* is open in the warmer months and contains memorabilia of early New England. The *American Precision Museum* has an interesting collection of hand and machine tools. Nearby *Mount Ascutney* is a popular family ski area.

WELLS WOOD

Route 12A, Plainfield, NH 03781. Mailing address: R.R. 2, Windsor, VT 05089. 603-675-5360. *Innkeepers*: Rosalind and Thomas Wells. Open all year.

Dating from 1895, Wells Wood was conceived and built by the great American illustrator and artist, Maxfield Parrish. This is a true baronial estate, part of the greater Cornish Art Colony which at one time had 450 resident painters, sculptors, writers, and actors. The inn has only four guest rooms, but each is quite spectacular. The master bedroom suite, for example, has a marble bath, a sitting room and a 20-mile view. The smallest bedroom is decorated with Delft tile. The common rooms of the inn include the Parchment Room, used for small gatherings; the Library, with fireplace and books for guests to read; the Acorn Room, a small dining room with low beams, brass and copper ornaments, and a fireplace; and the cocktail lounge, with its view of Mount Ascutney. Perhaps most spectacular is the Oak Room, once the music salon and now the main dining room of the inn. Paneled in oak with massive beams, it has a 14-foot wide fireplace and Palladian windows that look out upon Mount Ascutney and the Connecticut River Valley.

The restaurant at Wells Wood has received a great deal of acclaim. The menu is simple, with a choice of four appetizers, a soup of the day, and seven well-prepared entrees which currently include quiche Lorraine, chicken amandine, capon Cordon Bleu, crab Mornay, seafood Constantine, brochette de boeuf, and feast of Thomas (sirloin steak surrounded by mushrooms stuffed with shrimp). Dinners include soup, entree, salad, vegetables, relish tray, and bread and butter. Appetizers are additional. Dinner prices, without appetizer, range from $6.95 to $13.95. *Room Rates*: From $26.95 to $52.95 depending on room and season. No pets permitted. *Driving Instructions*: Take I-89 to exit 20. Then take Route 12A for 8½ miles to Wells Wood. Or, take I-91 to Route 12A and proceed north 9 miles to the inn.

NORTHERN

Chocorua, New Hampshire (see Tamworth, Sandwich, Chocorua)

STAFFORD'S-IN-THE-FIELD

Route 113, Chocorua, NH 03817. 603-323-7766. *Innkeepers*: Ramona and Fred Stafford. Open every day from Memorial Day to November, then open holiday weeks; from December 26 to April 1, open weekends only.

At the end of a picturesque country lane sits Stafford's-in-the-Field overlooking fields, forests, and a babbling brook. Built about 1778, the Federalist house had several additions made between the years of 1880 and 1905. The inn and its eight guest rooms are furnished with comfortable antiques. There are four guest cottages on the

property as well as a big old barn, Stafford's Barn, known for its good acoustics for string quartets and summer square dances. Guests eat family style at large tables in the dining room. Ramona is the chef, preparing many international dishes. For breakfast, guests might have blueberry-apple pancakes with the Stafford's own maple syrup, green chili omelets, eggs Benedict, and freshly baked currant muffins and warm breads. A dinner might include soup au Pistou and roast tenderloin with a Madeira sauce, followed by a rich dessert such as maple mousse or Brazilian orange cake.

To work off these meals, guests can square dance, swim in the old swimming hole in summer, or hike the long winding road that leads to Lake Chocorua with its view of Mount Chocorua. In the winter there is cross-country skiing on the property or at other nearby touring centers, plus a wide choice of alpine ski areas in the surrounding mountains. *Room Rates*: Double rooms, $29 to $32, MAP. Reservations are recommended. Children are welcome in summer only. No pets permitted. *Driving Instructions*: North on Route 93 to exit 23. Take Route 104 to Route 25; then go to Route 113. The inn is four miles down Route 113. If you are on Route 16 north, turn west onto Route 113 at Chocorua Village. The inn is one mile away.

Eaton Center, New Hampshire

Eaton Center is a small town south of Conway and near the edge of the *White Mountain National Forest*. The nearest ski area is *Mount Cranmore* in North Conway with its two skimobile tramways, three double chair lifts, and one Poma lift. For further information on the general region to the north of Eaton Center, see the White Mountain Region.

ROCKHOUSE MOUNTAIN FARM AND INN

Eaton Center, NH 03832. 603-447-2880. *Innkeepers*: The Edge Family. Open from June 15 through November 1.

The farm is located on the side of Rockhouse Mountain overlooking Crystal Lake, where the inn has its own private beach with boats. Operated for 31 years by the Edge family, the inn is designed for families who wish a complete farm vacation with horseback riding, barbecues, and even milking cows and feeding calves and piglets. There are 350 acres of wandering space for quiet hikes.

Breakfast and dinner are provided with a different home-cooked meal each night, always including freshly baked breads and rolls. The farmhouse, built in 1905, and barn, dating from the early 1800s, have modernized facilities. *Room Rates*: Single rooms, $25; double rooms, $19.50 to $22.50 per person, MAP. There are bunk rooms for teenagers at $13 to $18 per person. Weekly rates are available. No pets permitted. *Driving Instructions*: Six miles south of Conway, NH, on Route 153, take first right ¼ mile past post office.

Franconia, New Hampshire

Franconia is one of the White Mountain's most famous towns. Perhaps best known is the *Old Man of the Mountains*, the famous rock profile just south of the village. The *Cannon Mountain Ski Area* has a tramway that takes you to the top of the 4200-foot peak. The *League of New Hampshire Craftsmen* has an outlet in town. Another area favorite is the rock gorge, *The Flume*, to the south of the village. For further information on this area, see the White Mountains Region.

FRANCONIA INN

Route 116, Easton Road, Franconia, NH 03580. 800-258-8985 (in New Hampshire, call 823-5542). *Manager*: Dwight Blakeslee. Open Dec. 15 to April 15 and May 29 to Oct. 15.

For many years, there was a farm on the property that now houses the Franconia Inn. In the mid-1860s, the farm started to take boarders. By the early 1900s the farmhouse had been converted to a full tourist home and was being run as McKensie's. In 1934, however, a tremendous fire destroyed the original inn. Rebuilding started soon after, and the current structure was finished the following year. The inn ran successfully for many years but then closed. It was finally purchased and totally refurbished by Wade and Rachael Perry with the help of the Blakeslees.

The inn has 29 rooms with solid, comfortable furnishings. Some rooms have wood paneling and some are painted. Recreational facilities include a swimming pool, indoor and outdoor clay tennis courts, and 65 miles of cross-country ski trails, 40 of which are con-

tinually groomed. Meals are served in a spacious dining room, from a menu that changes daily. Each menu features 3 appetizers, 3 soups, and about 10 entrees. Dinner prices range from $7 to $11 for a complete meal. Typical dinner choices include fried pork tenderloin, veal cutlet aux champignons, Hungarian goulash, skewered lamb, stuffed fresh Boston scrod. Christmas dinner has included baked suckling pig as one of six entree choices. *Room Rates*: As a general rule, double rooms are from $24 to $40 per person, MAP. There are, however, a variety of rate structures and special packages. *Driving Instructions*: From the south take I-91 to the Wells River/Woodsville exit. Turn right on Route 302 to Lisbon, NH. A few miles past Lisbon, go right on Route 117 to Franconia. Crossing the bridge into town, go right to the Exxon station. There, turn right on Route 116 and go two miles to the inn. From Boston take I-93 to Lincoln, NH. Take Route 3 through Franconia Notch and then take Route I-93 again to exit 38 (Franconia). Turn left off the exit and cross the main road to Route 116. Proceed two miles to the inn.

LOVETT'S BY LAFAYETTE BROOK

Profile Road, Franconia, NH 03580. 603-823-7761. *Innkeeper*: Charles Lovett, Jr. Open Dec. 24–April 1, June 30–Oct. 9.
Lovett's is a semi-resort centered around a 170-year-old main inn and surrounded by several contemporary self-contained duplex units located in the pine woods around the property. The inn has much to appeal to a more mature clientele; however, there are numerous activities for children including Ping-Pong, pinball, and bumper pool. The main inn houses a comfortable bar, a sun-porch game room, a sitting room, and the dining room. Furnishings are generally colonial-style reproductions mixed with more contemporary pieces. The inn has its own swimming pool on ample grounds, which offer numerous views of the nearby White Mountains. Accommodations are varied and include both simple and spacious rooms in the inn, motel rooms, and others in the "Igloo Chalet," the "Yellow House," and "Stony Hill." *Room Rates*: Rates are complex due to the variety of accommodations. As a general guide, double rooms range in price from $16 to $38. MAP rates are also available. *Driving Instructions*: The inn is 2½ miles south of Franconia on Route 18.

141

Glen (see the White Mountains Region)

BERNERHOF INN

Route 302, Glen, NH 03838. 603-383-4414. *Innkeepers*: Ted and Sharon Weoblewski. Open all year.

The Bernerhof Inn was built in the early 1890s by a local businessman to serve travelers on their way to the Mount Washington Hotel. Since then it has been in continuous service as a hostelry, although ownership has changed several times. Its current name was coined about 1956 when new owners of Swiss background chose a name which means House of Bern. The inn is furnished with a number of antiques; a small, comfortable lounge and an intimate dining room contain Swiss and other European artifacts. The inn offers eight guest rooms which share bath facilities. Dinner is distinctly European with specialties such as delice de Gruyere, escargots Bourguignonne, Wiener schnitzel, piccata Bernerhof, fondue (both cheese and beef), and Hungarian goulash among the more than 20 appetizers and entrees. *Room Rates*: $16.75 per person, MAP, with several package plans available for longer stays. *Driving Instructions:* From Boston, take Route I-95 north to the Spaulding Turnpike. Then take Route 16 to Glen, where you turn left at Route 302 and proceed 1.5 miles to the inn, which is on the right.

Intervale (see the White Mountains Region)

HOLIDAY INN

Route 16A, Intervale, NH 03845. 603-356-9772. *Innkeepers*: Lois and Bob Gregory. Open from May 30 through fall foliage and then from December 26 through the skiing season.

Holiday Inn—no relation to the big chain—has been in continuous operation since the 1800s. Situated in the heart of Mount Washington Valley, with spacious grounds, mountain views, and a heated swimming pool, this small inn is a comfortable place. The rooms are furnished in the style of an old New Hampshire home with working fireplaces, flowered wallpaper, spindle beds, and crisp white curtains. Home-cooked meals are served family style and are available to guests and the public.

Holiday Inn has something for everyone: swimming and canoeing in the summer, hang gliding for the more adventurous, skating on the inn's lighted rink, cross-country skiing from the front door in winter. Thirteen rooms, seven with private bath. *Room Rates:* Double rooms, $17 to $20 per person, MAP; $12 to $15 per person with breakfast only. Mid-week discounts and package plans available. Reservations are advised. Small pets permitted in cottage only. *Driving Instructions:* 1½ miles on Route 16A, off Route 16 at north end of North Conway.

IDLEWILD INN

Intervale, NH 03845. 203-356-2752. *Innkeepers*: The Meserves and the Dinarelos. Open all year except for a few weeks in November.

In 1795, Captain Dinsmore received a license to "keep a publik house," and this was the beginning of the Idlewild Inn. The original house has, of course, changed considerably since then; several porches and wings have been added. Still, much of the original remains. In the center of the inn is the old keeping room, now the dining room. The old chimney, brick oven, fireplace, exposed corner posts, hand-hewn beams, and roof rafters have survived. The inn's 3 main rooms with working fireplaces and 10 guest rooms are furnished with antiques dating from 1750 to 1870.

The Idlewild serves breakfast and dinner to both guests and the public. Their specialties are Yankee pot roast and baked stuffed shrimp. *Room Rates*: Double rooms, $20 with private bath; $16 with shared bath. Mid-week discounts are available in ski season. No pets permitted. *Driving Instructions*: Can be reached via Route 16, 7, or 302, 1¾ miles north of North Conway.

THE NEW ENGLAND INN

Intervale, NH 03845. 603-356-5541. *Innkeepers*: Jerry and Betty Davis. Open all year. Dining room open from June to October 31 and from December 15 to March.

The New England grew into its innkeeping maturity slowly over the last 170 years. It began its life as the Bloodgood Farm, taking in road-weary travelers en route from Boston to Montreal. It provided them with a good bed, substantial meals, and a place for their horses. By the mid-1800s, the travelers were replaced at the farm by artists and other summer visitors. The White Mountain School of Art developed nearby, and even today the inn has paintings swapped for room and board. It has been modernized over the years, and most of the farm buildings have been converted into additional residences, but the modernization is not intrusive within the buildings. The farm grounds now offer a number of sports facilities including several excellent clay tennis courts (most of the big name pros who play at the Volvo Tennis Tournament practice here during that week), a four-hole golf course, and a pair of swimming pools. The buildings themselves have colonial decorations, making use of antiques wherever possible. The front parlors have fireplaces and there is a lounge in the ski barn. This is

not a small establishment. The complex consists of the main inn, Hampshire House, five duplex cottages, four single cottages, a motel unit, and the sports facilities already mentioned.

The inn serves a full country breakfast and a complete dinner every day. The dinner menu changes daily but often contains a dozen entree choices including lobster, steak, roasts, and fresh fish. All dinners include appetizer, soup, entree, salad, and dessert and are priced from about $6.25 to $9. One of the dessert specialties is ice cold lemon pie. *Room Rates*: Rates vary according to room selection and season. Rooms generally range from $20 to $37.50 per person, MAP, with weekly rates and special package plans available. Pets are permitted only in the cottages. *Driving Instructions*: The inn is on Route 16A, 3½ miles north of North Conway.

Jackson (see the White Mountains Region)

THORN HILL LODGE

Thorn Hill Road, Jackson Village, NH 03846. 603-383-4242. *Innkeepers*: Jacques and Carol Gagnon. Open from December to mid-April and from late May through October.

The Thorn Hill Lodge is an 1895 inn with a distinct Victorian feeling. The main building was recently augmented by four chalet buildings—three individual units and one with seven bedrooms. Thus, guests can choose between two distinct styles.

The main building contains a large living room with a well-stocked library. The papered walls, gold rugs, and fireplace give a warm feeling to this room with its large picture windows overlooking the Presidential Range. There are two dining rooms adjacent to the lounge. One is a dining porch with striking views of the mountains; the other has a country feeling in a Victorian setting. The inn maintains a waxing room in the basement for the many skiers who come here to enjoy the inn's access to three cross-country trails offering 125 km. of fine skiing on trails maintained by the Jackson Ski Touring Foundation. There is a large swimming pool for summer guests. The inn also offers special art workshops during July, September, and weekends in October.

Meals have a distinct New England flavor with daily specials including turkey, broiled sirloin, prime ribs of beef, or Yankee pot roast. There are also five regular dishes to choose from, including a vegetarian special of the day. Complete dinners with appetizer, entree, and beverage range in price from $6.50 to $10. In summer the inn maintains its own large vegetable garden which supplies fresh produce for the salads and vegetable dishes. *Room Rates*: $21 to $30 per person, MAP; $22 to $35 double occupancy, EP. Pets are permitted only in the three individual chalets. *Driving Instructions:* 1¼ miles past covered bridge, right on Thorn Hill Road to top of hill.

CHRISTMAS FARM INN

Route 16B, Jackson, NH 03846. 603-383-4313. *Innkeepers*: Bill and Sydna Zeliff. Open all year.

Christmas Farm Inn offers a variety of lodgings for skiers and other lovers of the good country life. The Main Inn, built in 1786, has comfortable colonial guest rooms and dining and living rooms with fireplaces. The other guest quarters include a Log Cabin, a 1771 Salt Box, and a converted Maple Sugaring House. All of these have spectacular views of Attitash and 11 other surrounding peaks. The dining room menu features hearty skiers' breakfasts, as well as homemade stews, soups, and freshly baked breads and pastries.

For the cross-country skiers, some of Jackson's 125 km. of trails begin right at the inn. All trail fees are provided, as well as a waxing room and trail lunches. There is also a free shuttle to nearby areas. *Room Rates*: $18 to $30 per person, MAP. The inn also offers numerous packages for all seasons and amounts of time. Reservations are required. Pets are not encouraged. *Driving Instructions*: Route 16 north, through North Conway, over the covered bridge into Jackson Village (16A). Follow signs to the inn.

THE WILDCAT INN AND TAVERN

Route 16, Jackson, NH 03846. 603-383-4245. *Innkeeper*: Bradford L. Boynton. Open from June to October and from December to April.

The Wildcat is a nineteenth-century inn with period antiques as part of its decor. There are two fireplaces in the taproom, one in the reading room, and an old parlor stove in the dining room. Many guests are drawn to the area by the Jackson Touring Foundation cross-country skiing trails and by the exciting downhill ski-

146

ing at *Tuckerman's Ravine* and *Wildcat Mountain*. The inn offers accommodations for 40 guests in private guest rooms or in small bunk rooms. It also has a recreation room with television and games. The village skating rink is just across the road.

The inn serves three meals a day to guests and the general public. Dinners feature a selection of appetizers, soups, and choice of entree, including steak, shashlik, sautéed veal, lasagna, seafood, crepes, and a vegetarian loaf. Prices for meals are a la carte. *Room Rates*: $10 to $14 per person, plus a 15 percent charge for gratuities and 6 percent state tax. *Driving Instructions*: Jackson is on Route 16 about a dozen miles north of Conway.

North Conway (see the White Mountains Region)

NERELEDGE INN

River Road, North Conway, NH 03860. Mailing Address: Box 432, North Conway, NH 03860. 603-356-2831. *Innkeepers*: Marti and Steve Gourley. Open from May 30 to October 15 and from November 20 to Easter.

The Nereledge Inn, built in 1787, has 2 parlors (one with fireplace), a dining room, and 11 guest rooms that share 3 baths. The dining room has a panoramic view of the Saco River, Intervale, and the White Horse and Cathedral ledges. Many of the rooms contain antiques or attractive reproductions.

The inn is known locally for its hearty breakfasts, always including home-fried potatoes and hot apple pie, which are a real buy.

Dinners are also a bargain. A 16-ounce broiled sirloin steak is $5.95; other items include shrimp, pork chops, scallops, roast beef, liver and onions, and spaghetti or lasagna. In addition to the regular menu, there is a daily special—usually a roast dish priced from $3.95 to $4.95. *Room Rates*: Double rooms are $14 per person, MAP, or $8 per person, EP. Single rooms are $1 more per person. Skiing package plans are available. No pets permitted. *Driving Instructions*: The inn is 300 feet from Route 16 on River Road in North Conway.

Pittsburg, New Hampshire (including Colebrook and the Connecticut Lakes Region)

Pittsburg is the fishing and hunting headquarters for this area. In 1832, during a border dispute between Canada and the United States, an independent nation was declared here called the Indian Stream Territory. In the area there are the three Connecticut lakes plus man-made Lake Francis. The 45th parallel passes nearby, marking the spot equidistant from the equator and the North Pole.

To the south, Colebrook is situated in the shadow of Mount Monadnock. Set in a great logging area, the town now has a modern shopping center and a small airport. The area also provides golf on three courses, hunting, fishing, and canoeing. In addition, it is a photographer's and artist's paradise. The *Wilderness Ski Area* at Dixville Notch has both downhill and cross-country skiing.

THE GLEN LODGE

First Connecticut Lake, Pittsburg, NH 03592. 603-538-6500. *Innkeeper*: Mrs. Betty H. Falton. Open from May 15 to early October.

The main lodge here was built in 1900 as a private lake-shore lodge and retreat. It soon became a fishing resort. In 1947, 10 cottages were added that variously accommodate two to eight persons. Staying here is rather like visiting a private wilderness estate. The cottages have rustic log exteriors and wood paneling inside. The main lodge also has a rustic feeling with its working fireplaces and sturdy pine furniture. Both lake and stream fishing are available, and the catch might include landlocked salmon, lake trout, rainbow trout, brown trout, and squaretails. The staff will be happy to arrange fishing trips in more remote waters for the adventurous.

The dining room serves three meals daily to both guests and public, with home-baked breads, pies, and cakes, as well as a salad bar. There is a weekly buffet and cookouts are optional at lunch. The lodge is a relaxing place without organized social activity. Its great appeal is to lovers of sports and nature, and to those who just want to be away from the more organized tourist scene. *Room Rates*: $24 to $32. Pets are permitted. *Driving Instructions*: U.S. 93 or 95 to Route 3 in Lancaster, NH. Then north through Pittsburg village 10 miles. The lodge is a mile off the highway on a private road. Call up for detailed instructions.

Tamworth, Sandwich, Chocorua (see also the Dartmouth–Lake Sunapee Region)

The town of Tamworth was established in 1766. Logging is and has been important to the area since before the Revolution when masts for the king's ships were hauled down "Old Mast Road" by ox cart. Most of the villages in the area have remained relatively untouched for the past 100 years.

Today, it is a quiet section of the state known to tourists primarily for hiking and mountain climbing, including the relatively easy and popular *Mount Chocorua*. No special equipment is required for completing this hike although many visitors camp out near the summit. *The Barnstormers Theater* in Tamworth is the oldest summer theater in the state and is directed by the son of President Grover Cleveland who had a summer home there. Auctions are held frequently in the warmer months next to the Tamworth Inn. There are dog-sled races in the area in January and a number of cross-country skiing trails nearby. *The Hemenway State Forest* is just north of Tamworth and the *White Lake State Park* is in Tamworth itself and offers swimming, fishing, hiking, picnicking, and camping. In summer months there is square dancing at *Stafford's Barn* in Chocorua. A country fair is held annually in Sandwich each Columbus Day. Sandwich is also the home of the original building set up by the *League of New Hampshire Craftsmen*.

TAMWORTH INN

Main Street, Tamworth, NH 03886. 603-323-7721. *Innkeepers*: Bill and Sue McCarthy and Doug and Linda Conway. Open all year, but it is suggested that you call in advance to make sure.

The Tamworth was first constructed in 1830, with additions made from 1870 through 1900; it has been an inn since 1888. It has a pub room with entertainment on weekends. The pub and the living room both have working fireplaces and many antiques. Cross-country ski equipment may be rented and used on the many natural trails to be found here. The inn has its own pool and there is excellent trout fishing nearby. This is an area of few crowds and warm hospitality. During the summer months the local theater draws interested spectators from other parts of the state.

Meals are chosen from a simple menu consisting of eight entrees, including scallops Tamworth ($5.95), roast turkey ($4.50),

and steak au poivre ($7.95). *Room Rates*: Double rooms, $15 to $27. The inn also offers winter packages which include three-night stays for the price of two, or five-night stays for the price of three. Rooms are available MAP, from $18 per person for a room without private bath to $22.50 per person for a suite with bath. Package plans are also available for guests choosing MAP. Pets are permitted. *Driving Instructions*: Take Route I-93 north of Concord and Laconia to exit 23. Take Route 104 east to Route 3 and then take that a short distance to Route 25 and continue northeast to Whittier, where you take Route 113 north into Tamworth.

Thornton, New Hampshire (including Campton) (see the White Mountains Region)

AMITY HOUSE

Route 49, Thornton, NH. Mailing Address: RFD #1 Campton, NH 03223. 603-726-9881. *Innkeepers*: Peter and Carolyn Wolfe. Open from July 1 to October 30 and Thanksgiving to April 1.

Amity House is a friendly little country inn, offering five guest rooms with shared baths and three small bunk rooms that appeal most to winter skiers and summer hikers who are attracted to the Waterville Valley area. Children have fun exploring the woods, river, swimming hole, and the working farm nearby. The inn itself is a renovated farmhouse with a fieldstone fireplace, braided rugs, wide board floors in the dining room and bedrooms, a few antiques, and lots of books and paintings. In the summer, the Wolfes put fresh flowers in every room. They work hard to cultivate their flower beds and a small organic garden. Combined with the friendly spirit and informal atmosphere is a touch of elegance here and there. Guests dine by candlelight and are invited to bring their own wine. The menu changes daily and usually includes a choice of at least two entrees. A recent dinner menu offered fresh mushroom soup, fettucine Alfredo, broiled fresh salmon steak or sauté de veau au calvados, salad, homemade bread, and a fresh fruit tart. The full dinner price was either $8.95 (for the salmon) or $9.50 (for the veal). *Room Rates*: Double rooms, $17 per person; bunk rooms, $13 per person, both MAP. No pets permitted.

Driving Instructions: Exit 28 off I-93, bear right towards Waterville Valley to Goose Hollow (about 4 miles). Inn on left at intersection.

The White Mountains Region (including Campton, Conway, Franconia, Glen, Gorham, Intervale, Jackson, Jefferson, Lincoln, Littleton, North Conway, Twin Mountain, and Woodstock, New Hampshire)

This region of New Hampshire probably has more tourist attractions than any comparable area in New England. Among the many popular sights are the *Attitash Alpine Slide* in Bartlet; the spectacular *Gondola Rides* at Wildcat Mountain, Loon Mountain, and Cannon Mountain; the *Conway Scenic Railroad* with its old-time train ride; *Storyland* at Glen, NH, with its castle, storybook adventures, and people; the brand new *Heritage-New Hampshire* adjacent to Storyland; and the *Polar Caves*, New Hampshire's natural wonder left over from the days of glaciers. There is also *Santa's Village* outside Jefferson, *Six Gun City* in Jefferson, and the *Flume* at Franconia Notch.

The White Mountain National Forest has 730,000 acres of mountains and deep forest with numerous camp grounds, hiking trails, and ski areas including *Wildcat, Loon, Waterville Valley, Attitash,*

Cannon Mountain, Black Mountain, Bretton Woods, Tyrol, and *Mount Cranmore.* In addition, there are more than 15 ski touring centers, and the area is the home of the Appalachian Mountain Club which operates numerous mountain huts for hikers and skiers. The rivers provide excellent canoeing, although several are rated as difficult and must be approached with caution. Most of the ski areas are surrounded by numerous shops and restaurants. The *League of New Hampshire Craftsmen* operates branch outlets in Franconia and North Conway.

No visit to this region would be complete without a trip to the top of Mount Washington via either the *Mount Washington Auto Road* (in warm months; a toll is charged) or the *Mount Washington Cog Railway.*

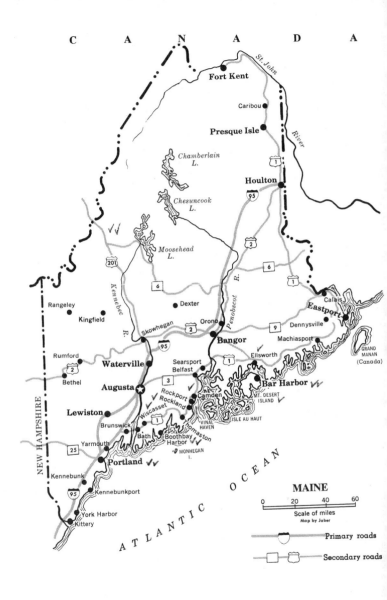

C A N A D A

Fort Kent

Caribou

Presque Isle

Chamberlain L.

Houlton

Chesuncook L.

St. John River

Moosehead L.

Rangeley

Kingfield

Dexter

Skowhegan

Orono

Bangor

Calais

Eastport

Dennysville

Machiasport

GRAND MANAN
(Canada)

Rumford

Waterville

Searsport

Belfast

Ellsworth

Bethel

Augusta

Camden

Bar Harbor

Lewiston

Rockport
Rockland

MT. DESERT
ISLAND

Brunswick

Wiscasset

ISLE AU HAUT

Bath

VINAL
HAVEN

Yarmouth

Thomaston

Boothbay
Harbor

Portland

MONHEGAN
I.

Kennebunk

Kennebunkport

York Harbor

Kittery

NEW HAMPSHIRE

Kennebec R.

Penobscot R.

ATLANTIC OCEAN

MAINE

0   20   40   60

Scale of miles
Map by Jaber

Primary roads

Secondary roads

Maine

MAINE is no stranger to visitors. Inhabited by a number of American Indian tribes for thousands of years, the first European visitors to the area were probably explorers connected to the early Norwegian explorations headed by Leif Ericson around the year 1000. Some 500 years later, Giovanni da Verrazano, the great Italian navigator, landed here and there along the Maine coastline. But in 1604 Sieur de Monts made the first settlement north of St. Augustine, Florida, on Neutral Island, at the mouth of the St. Croix River; the settlement moved to Nova Scotia after one winter.

Much of Maine was originally owned by Massachusetts, though the more northern portions were claimed by France. The French claim was contested in a number of bloody French and Indian wars until 1760, when the final surrender and treaty turned over the control of the land area that is now Maine to Massachusetts. The timber riches of this vast area provoked continuing disputes over the exact location of the Canadian border. These disputes were finally settled by the War of 1812 and later border treaties. Finally, Maine seceded from Massachusetts in 1819 and was granted statehood the following year. Gradually, new industries were added to those of timber and fur, primarily fishing, lobstering, quarrying, farming, and ship building. All these industries today remain major sources of revenue in Maine. For many years, however, another important industry has been tourism.

Most visitors to Maine never really comprehend the magnitude of this state. To more fully grasp Maine's size, it is necessary to realize that all five other New England states could almost fit into the state of Maine. Furthermore, much of the East Coast's lumber, a large percentage of its annual potato crop, its blueberries, and nearly all of its lobsters are produced in Maine. This is the land of thousands of lakes, millions of acres of forest, and over two thousand miles of ocean and tidal coastline. Maine was, until recently, known almost exclusively to tourists for its coastal features.

Gradually, however, interest has grown in the interior regions with their extensive fishing, hunting, and lakeside recreation. The advent of Maine skiing, both downhill and cross-country, has brought thousands of winter sports' enthusiasts to the state. Snowmobiling here is not only a sport, but a practical means of transportation for many. This year-round attractiveness is gradually being reflected by Maine's inns, which are staying open longer and longer.

Visitors to Maine can get excellent advance vacation-planning help from two sources within the state: the Maine Publicity Bureau is a privately funded promotional organization which will be happy to mail potential visitors an excellent packet of information. Its address is Maine Publicity Bureau, 1 Gateway Circle, Portland, ME 04101. Its phone number is 207-773-7266. The Maine State Chamber of Commerce also provides excellent information. Write to it at 477 Congress Street, Portland, ME 04111. In addition, many areas have roadside information booths to help travelers. Some of these are open in the summer months only.

COASTAL

Blue Hill, Maine (see also Deer Isle)

Blue Hill is an old town with white clapboard homes set at the base of Blue Hill, a nine-hundred-foot hill topped with a fire tower and affording a spectacular view of the bay and its islands, as well as a beautiful cove. The town has many craft shops including the two well-known potteries, *Roantrees* and *Rackcliffe*. The *Kneisel Hall Music School*'s Chamber Players give concerts every Wednesday and Saturday night and Sunday afternoon throughout the summer. The school was founded by violinist Franz Kneisel. The *Blue Hill Country Club* has a nine-hole golf course open to the public. In South Blue Hill one can see the reversing tidal falls. Acadia National Park (offering cross-country skiing in winter), Deer Isle, Isle au Haut, and Bar Harbor can all be reached by day trips from Blue Hill.

BLUE HILL INN

Blue Hill, ME 04614. 207-374-2844. *Innkeepers*: Jean and Fred Wakelin. Open all year.

The Blue Hill, built in 1830, has been in operation as an inn since 1840. It is an old white clapboard building with many chimneys and huge shade trees. The bright and cheery rooms are cooled by ocean breezes in summer and warmed by crackling fires in wood-burning stoves in the cooler months. The eight guest rooms are filled with a blend of antiques and comfortable furniture. An old grandfather's clock presides over the living room. Gingham-check and flowered wallpapers in the rooms and crisp white curtains at the many-paned windows add a country charm to the old inn.

There is no regular menu but the Wakelins serve a different home-cooked meal each day plus a choice of lobster or steak. Breakfast and dinner are served to guests and the public. Guests may bring their own liquor since there is no liquor license at present. Blue Hill Country Club extends privileges of tennis, golf, and its beach to guests of the inn. *Room Rates*: June 1 through Labor Day, single rooms, $24; double rooms, $30. Off season, single, $18; double, $24. Reservations recommended especially June through November. No pets permitted. *Driving Instructions*: Maine Turnpike (I-95) to Augusta. Take Route 3 past Bucksport, then turn right onto Route 15 and proceed to Blue Hill.

√Boothbay Harbor, Maine

Boothbay Harbor is a jewel along the rockbound coast of Maine. The Boothbay Harbor area was first visited by Captain John Smith, who landed on Monhegan Island, a short distance from the harbor area, in the year 1616. Today, it is a very active harbor with many fishing boats, and is the home of the *Windjammer Days* parade of old schooners in mid-July. Visitors exploring this village are encouraged to visit the *Boothbay Railway Museum* to ride on the country's only steam-operated, two-foot-gauge railroad and to see the museum's many other fine collections of transportation memorabilia. Also in Boothbay Harbor is *Hyde House*, home of the Boothbay Region Historical Society, and the *Grand Banks Schooner Museum*. More than 40 cruise and fishing expeditions now leave from Boothbay Harbor at different times.

THE THISTLE INN

53 Oak Street, Boothbay Harbor, ME 04538. 207-633-3541. *Innkeeper*: Leonie Greenwood-Adams. Open all year.

This street-front inn in the center of the village is both a popular tourist attraction and a favorite haunt of the local fishermen and lobstermen. This is undoubtedly due to the immense popularity of the innkeeper, Leonie Greenwood-Adams, who has described herself as a "surly proprietress." She has, in fact, created an extremely friendly inn where a strong Scottish influence prevails in a 145-year-old former home of a sea captain. Lunch and dinner are served in the restaurant and the menu includes scallops flambé ($7.95), T'Donalds Scottish lobster pie ($8.50), and a house steak with mushroom and lobster sauce ($11) among the many meat and seafood offerings. There is a popular dory bar which is often the loudest place in the town, especially when all the lobster boats are in at the same time. The inn has 10 rooms, only 1 with a private bath. Rooms are decorated with New England furniture dating from the late 1800s. *Room Rates*: $9.45 to $18.90 during the summer season; $8.40 to $14.70 from Labor Day to June 1. Pets are permitted. *Driving Instructions*: U.S. Route 1 to Route 27 south to Boothbay Harbor.

CLIPPER INN

94 Commercial Street, Boothbay Harbor, ME 04538. 207-633-5152. *Innkeeper*: Fredrick J. Hughes. Open all year.

The Clipper, a small waterfront inn, has 33 rooms with private baths as well as a restaurant with a view of the harbor and a roar-

ing fire on cool days. Guests at the inn are automatically enrolled in the Boothbay Harbor YMCA, which has excellent recreational facilities including tennis, handball, racquet ball, and pool. Of special interest, according to innkeeper Fred Hughes, is the fact that the inn seems to be haunted "by the ghost of a young bride whose husband disappeared on her wedding night. One small third floor of the inn has been shut off completely because of this. There is no longer a staircase leading to it—the only access is through the walls." All this adds to the romantic atmosphere of the inn. *Room Rates*: Double rooms start at $26 in the summer and at $22 in the off season. There is a "Getaway Anyday" package available from October 1 to June 1 at $19.50 per person per day, MAP. Pets are permitted. *Driving Instructions*: From Wiscassett (on U.S. 1) take Route 27 south to Boothbay Harbor.

LINEKIN BAY RESORT

Wall Point Road, Boothbay Harbor, ME 04538. Winter Address: 61 Meadow Street, Florence, MA 01063. 207-633-2494. *Innkeepers*: Robert and Ida Branch. Open from mid-June through Labor Day.

The Linekin Bay is not an inn; rather, it is a first-class resort consisting of 75 rooms and 40 buildings. It is included here because of its reputation as a summer resort, and because it gives the reader some variety of choice in vacation places. The resort adds no extra charges for the use of any of its extensive facilities which include swimming in the heated saltwater pool overlooking the bay, sailing with appropriate instruction in the largest resort sailing fleet in

159

New England, canoeing, water skiing (with instruction provided), tennis, fishing, and shuffleboard. Three meals are served daily and include a variety of Maine seafood including lobster cookouts beside the pool. Accommodations are provided in a choice of 5 lodges and 30 cabins that are scattered among the pine trees. *Room Rates*: All-inclusive rates range from $19 to $28 per person, AP, with 10 percent discounts in June. No pets permitted. *Driving Instructions*: From the east side of Boothbay Harbor, turn left at the Catholic Church. Follow Lobster Cove Road to Wall Point Road. The resort is at the end of Wall Point Road.

SPRUCEWOLD LODGE

Boothbay Harbor, ME 04538. 207-633-3600. *Innkeeper*: John M. McQuade. Open from July 1 to September 1.

The Sprucewold Lodge is a modest-sized log cabin style structure offering 29 rooms, all with private bath. Some rooms are found within one of their two additional separate log cabins. The lodge, built in 1925, offers on-the-grounds tennis, swimming in the pool or in the waters off the beach (for those hardy enough to brave the chilling Maine waters), shuffleboard, and Ping-Pong. The lodge offers "A Maine Interlude" of four days and three nights with all breakfasts and dinners (including a lobster and steak barbecue), a cruise along the coast on board the M/V *Goodtime*, and sightseeing at Pemaquid Point. *Room Rates*: Rates start at $25. The log cabin cottages are rented on a weekly basis. The "Maine Interlude" package plan is available to tour groups of 40 or more and costs $119 per person. *Driving Instructions*: Take Route 27 south to Boothbay Harbor and follow the signs to the lodge.

Brooksville, West Brooksville, and Sargentville (see Blue Hill, Maine, and Deer Isle, Maine)

OAKLAND HOUSE

Herrick Road, Brooksville, ME. Mailing Address: Sargentville, ME 04673. 207-359-8521. *Innkeeper*: James Littlefield. Open from June 20 to September 10 with full facilities, and for six weeks before and after these dates without the dining room.

Nestled between Lake Winnewaug and Penobscot Bay, the Oakland House was built as a private residence prior to 1776. Additions were made in 1889 so as to create a house with rooms for rent. The inn was originally a resting place for travelers who arrived by steamship that landed at Herrick's Landing. Over the years, a number of cottages have been built, so at the present time a guest can choose the more old-fashioned rooms in Oakland House itself or the privacy of one of the 10 family cottages. In addition, there is an Annex which has a living room with fireplace, three guest rooms and bath on the first floor, and four guest rooms and a bath on the upper floor. There is also a detached building called Shore Oaks with 10 large guest rooms (2 with fireplaces).

Meals are served in the main house and feature lobster, clams, crabmeat, and fresh fish dishes, plus homemade pastries, desserts, and rolls. Weekly features are the lobster picnic on the beach every Thursday evening and the Sunday buffet which always includes a lobster dish.

The inn could be described as a low-key resort. Activities are not pushed on guests, but there is much to do here. It is unusual in that it has access both to saltwater bathing from its own private beach and to fresh water bathing on the shore of Lake Winnewaug. The inn provides rowboats for both types of water at no extra charge. Sailboats may be rented nearby for longer visits and moored at Oakland House. *Room Rates*: June 20 to September 10, $115.50 to $217 per person per week, AP. During off season, the cottages are available for rental for $125 per cottage per week, without meals. Pets are permitted. *Driving Instructions*: Take Route 15 south approximately 12 miles from Blue Hill to the inn's sign on the right. (If you come to a large green suspension bridge you have passed the turn by ¾ mile.)

DAVID'S FOLLY

Route 176, West Brooksville, ME. Mailing Address: R.R. #2, Brooksville, ME 04617. 207-326-8834. *Innkeepers*: The Cutler Family. Open from mid-June to October 1.

The inn consists of a white main building connected by a converted woodshed to an old barn. There is a huge living room with two bay windows, a library for relaxing, and, in the barn, a recreation room and lounge. The Cutlers purchased the farm in 1939 and restored it to its original beauty.

The dining room serves farm-fresh food family style, with everything made from scratch. Some of the daily specials include fresh fish on Tuesdays, a cookout on Wednesdays (weather permitting), boiled lobster on Fridays, and a roast of either lamb, beef, or turkey on Sundays. The inn sometimes serves a real New England boiled dinner as well as other New England specialties—Indian pudding, coffee jelly, johnnycake and homemade pickles. The kitchen's black iron stove is still used to bake the traditional Saturday night baked beans, raisin brown bread, and blueberry pie.

David's Folly is a saltwater farm. The fields slope gently to the inn's private cove where guests can swim, fish, dig for clams, and row out to the nearby islands to explore. The guest rooms are spread out between the main house, the converted woodshed, the barn, and a separate cabin. Some rooms have private baths and some share baths. *Room Rates*: Rooms with semiprivate baths, $150 per person per week; rooms with private baths, $159 per person per week; and $168 per person per week for the cabin which has twin bedrooms, bath, and a small living room with wood-burning iron stove, all AP. Daily rates range from $28 to $30 per person. The cabin is rented only on a weekly basis. Pets are permitted in the barn rooms and cabin only. *Driving Instructions*: Take Maine Turnpike to Augusta and then Route 3 to Bucksport and Route 15 to North Penobscot, where you turn left onto Route 199 to Penobscot. Turn right from Route 199 onto Route 175. Follow Route 175 to North Brooksville, where you turn right onto Route 176. The inn is four miles ahead in West Brooksville.

√Camden, Maine

This classic harbor town in mid-coast Maine is set on the slopes of the Camden Hills that descend into the harbor itself. Visitors to this area may use Camden as a base to explore the mid-coast region, including *Camden Hills State Park*; the *Old Conway House and Museum*; numerous scenic cruises on Penobscot Bay; and the famed *Windjammer Cruises* along coastal Maine, many departing from this port. This village has easy access along Route 1 to the nearby towns of Lincolnville to the north and to Rockport and Rockland to the south. Winter visitors will enjoy using the skiing facilities of the *Camden Snow Bowl* and *Ragged Mountain*. Golfers have use of the *Goose River Golf Course* and the *Rockland Golf Club* in nearby Rockland. Camden also provides a scenic base for those who wish to attend the immensely popular *Maine Seafood Festival* held in Rockland during the first weekend in August each year. A short trip inland will bring visitors to our favorite country fair in Union, usually held the third weekend in August.

CAMDEN HARBOUR INN

83 Bayview Street, Camden, ME 04843. 207-236-4200. *Innkeepers*: Jim and Loureen Gilbert. Open all year except from April 15 to May 15.

The Camden Harbour Inn has 18 rooms in a sturdy-looking Victorian (1892) building with a wraparound porch. Nine of these rooms share baths while the other nine have private baths, all with the original clawfoot tubs. Comfort here is old-fashioned, without the addition of modern conveniences like television or room telephones. The restaurant specializes in seafood, steaks, chops, and prime rib roasts. *Room Rates*: June 1 to November 1, from $18 for a single with shared bath to $28.50 for a double with private bath

and "a view." Rates during the remainder of the year are about 20 percent lower. Pets are permitted. *Driving Instructions*: Take U.S. 1 to the center of Camden, then go along Bayview Street three blocks to the inn.

Deer Isle, Maine

Deer Isle is a jewel of an island in Penobscot Bay, not too far from Bar Harbor, *Acadia National Park*, and the village of Blue Hill. Deer Isle was first settled in 1763 while Maine was still part of the Massachusetts Colony. Early occupations included farming, ice cutting, and stone quarrying, but lobstering was and still is the major industry here. Another important industry is tourism. The island was linked to the mainland by bridge in 1938. The Deer Isle-Stonington Historical Society operates an historic house and museum called *Aust Salome Sellers*. Here visitors can see collections of local artifacts, as well as an Indian collection.

PILGRIM'S INN

Main Street, Deer Isle, ME 04627. 207-348-6615. *Innkeepers*: George and Eleanor Pavloff. Open from April 1 to December 1. In 1793, Ignatius Haskell built one of the most impressive homes on Deer Isle. The owner of a thriving sawmill, Haskell was a framer of the constitution of the state of Maine. Now Pilgrim's Inn, it has a true colonial flavor with its pumpkin pine wide-board floors, soft colonial tones on the walls, paneled parlor, and numerous working fireplaces. Guests can sit in the common room and gaze out over the mill pond nearby. Before-dinner cocktails and hors d'oeuvres are also served in this room. The inn currently has eight guest rooms, all but one with semiprivate baths.

Dining room meals are enhanced by a specialty at the inn—open-hearth cooking. Whenever possible roasts and fowl are cooked in a hearth oven in front of a 7½-foot fireplace. Dinners do not follow a set menu but are selected according to the freshest ingredients available. A typical recent dinner included avocados stuffed with shrimp, poisson à l'Orientale (marinated in ginger, orange, and soy sauce, and then broiled), vegetables from the inn garden, rice pilaf, homemade French bread, garden salad, blueberry pie, coffee, and cheese. *Room Rates*: $35 per person or $225 per person weekly, both MAP. Guests at the inn have guest privileges at the Island Country Club. Pets are permitted. *Driving Instructions*: From Boston drive north on I-95; at Brunswick take Route 1. Past Bucksport turn right on Route 15 to Deer Isle Village. There, turn right on Main Street (the Sunset Road) and drive one block to the inn on the left-hand side of the road.

Dennysville and surrounding Washington County

Washington County is the last frontier on the East Coast of the United States. A county of tremendous size, its area is larger than the combined states of Rhode Island and Delaware. It has over 1½ million acres and includes 133,000 acres of lakes left by the action of three successive glacial invasions. This is a sports paradise as well as a welcome retreat from the crowds of more southern Maine. The county produces the largest crop of blueberries annually in the world. There are two cities of note: Calais, pronounced locally as "Cal-luss," and Machias, pronounced Mach-EYE-us. Calais is on the Canadian border and has a special bond of friendship with its Canadian sister city, St. Stephen. Calais imports all its drinking water from across the border and fires in either city are answered by fire-fighting forces from both cities. The *St. Croix Historical Society* has its headquarters here.

The *Thomas Ruggles House* in Columbia Falls has carved flutings and beadings and a fine flying staircase. The house, preserved in its original form, is open daily to the public.

Machias is the shire town of the county and is noted for its fine white houses lining the Machias River, which opens into a salt bay via a series of rugged ledges. Machias was the scene of the first naval battle in the Revolutionary War when the British schooner *Margaretta* was captured by land forces from the American side. The *Burnham Tavern* survives today from that period. It is maintained and kept open to the public by the DAR.

Dennysville and West Pembroke are small neighboring towns filled with New England white clapboard homes. The Dennys River is a popular swimming, boating, and salmon-fishing spot. West Pembroke is the location of the famous Reversing Falls, where the saltwater rushes in to meet the fresh water.

Other towns in this large county include Woodland, with its enormous industrial complex at the St. Croix Paper Co., a division of Georgia Pacific; Eastport, with its two sardine canneries; and Lubec, with the Roosevelt Cottage on Campobello Island. There is an excellent country club on St. Croix Island. This island (also called Neutral Island) was the scene of the second European settlement in the New World (after St. Augustine, Florida). Samuel de Champlain spent the winter of 1604 in this area, which has been made a national monument.

LINCOLN HOUSE

Dennysville, ME 04628. 207-726-3953. *Innkeepers*: Mary Carol and Jerry Haggerty. Open all year.

At the end of the Revolutionary War, Benjamin Lincoln accepted the sword of surrender from General Cornwallis. He then was permitted by General Washington to purchase 10,000 acres of land in northern Maine (at that time part of Massachusetts). In 1787, Mr. Lincoln built a fine country house of 15 rooms on the property.

The inn has had a rich history in its 190 years. Indians often received lodging in the summer kitchen of the inn and John James Audubon was a guest there for two weeks on his way to Newfoundland. (Audubon was so pleased with his two-week stay at the Lincoln's home that he named a sparrow the Lincoln sparrow.)

In late 1976, the Haggerty's purchased the old home and began to carefully return it to its former splendor. The process has been a slow one because Jerry Haggerty, a restorer of antiques, is a perfectionist and insists on restoring rather than renovating.

The result is a simple elegance which has been recreated in a fine country home. There are two dining rooms, a main kitchen and a summer one, and six comfortable guest rooms. From several guest rooms you can see the river below, with its family of nesting eagles. In the winter it is currently the only inn open in Washington County.

Mary Carol Haggerty takes great care in the supervision of the cooking at the inn. Dinners, served to the guests and, with advance reservations, to the public, are always single-entree affairs and begin with homemade soups like a lentil with croutons or a cream of crab. Soups are followed by generous servings of the main entree which might be roast beef, roast pork, coq au vin. haddock soufflé, or braised beef and mushrooms. The entree always is served with homemade bread, vegetables, and a salad. Desserts include a variety of homemade cakes and pies. Dinner prices vary, according to entree, from $8 to $10 complete.

The Haggertys are gradually expanding a plan to offer fine antiques for sale at the inn. Carefully restored pieces are placed in the inn itself where they can do service until they are admired by a guest and purchased. In this way antique lovers can see a limited selection of pieces in a functional setting. *Room Rates*: Single rooms, $20; double, $30. A full breakfast is available to guests for $3. *Driving Instructions*: From Bangor, take Route 1A to Ellsworth, then take Route 1 to Dennysville. The inn is within sight of the intersection of Route 1 and Route 86 in Dennysville.

Islesboro, Maine

Islesboro is a secluded island in the middle of Penobscot Bay, three miles off the coast at Lincolnville Beach, north of Camden. It is largely a summer community of substantial homes with few activities and little provision for a tourist population. Because access is by a ferry which follows a limited daily schedule, island road traffic is kept to a minimum. There are few shops other than those that serve the island's summer residents. This is a lovely island to visit if you are lucky enough to be a guest at a home here or in one of its few inns. The island ferry dock and public boat launching area serve boaters who wish to gain access to *Warren Island State Park*, which is accessible only to campers who arrive by boat. This area provides the only camping on Islesboro. Day visitors are encouraged to take a leisurely drive around the island to enjoy the spectacular scenery and to explore or relax on the beaches.

ISLESBORO INN

Islesboro, ME 04848. *Innkeeper*: Mrs. Doris T. Anderson. 207-734-2221. Open from mid-June to mid-October.

The Islesboro Inn describes itself as a converted "summer cottage." The magnitude of this understatement can be determined when the reader learns that this "cottage" has twelve working fireplaces. Indeed, seven of these are located in guest rooms and the remaining ones in various public rooms that boast spectacular views of Penobscot Bay. Even the ride to the island is a treat aboard the *Governor Muskie*, a 24-car, 125-passenger ferry that leaves from the small harbor at Lincolnville. As you watch the

mainland slip away, you are easily convinced that a time of great relaxation is ahead. The inn has a lovely terrace often used for luncheon as well as cocktails before dinner. There are six guest moorings for yachts reserved next door at the nine-hole golf course that is open to the public. The inn also has a clay-surfaced tennis court. Life at the inn is purposely slow and relaxing, and the separation of the island from the mainland means that guests are more likely to be contented with sailing, bicycling, bird-watching, berry picking, or beachcoming. However, day trips to the mainland and nearby Lincolnville, Camden, and Rockland will provide ample opportunity to go shopping or to explore the many fine local restaurants. There is an excellent informal lobster house right near the entrance to the ferry at Lincolnville Beach, where you can eat inexpensive shore dinners on picnic tables outdoors or in somewhat more formal settings inside. Visitors to the island are warned, however, that the ferry schedule is strictly adhered to and it is possible to be stranded on the wrong side of the bay if you let time slip by unnoticed. *Room Rates*: From $40 (with shared bath) to $50 *per person* per day, MAP. No pets permitted. *Driving Instructions*: Take U.S. Route 1 north of Rockland through Camden and to Lincolnville Beach. Board the ferry there; upon disembarking on Islesboro Island, take the first three right-hand turns in a row. There is a sign on the tree at the third right.

Kennebunkport, Maine

Kennebunkport is a typical Maine seacoast harbor town. Much of the village has remained untouched for over 100 years. This area has long been a favorite of vacationers and is somewhat crowded during the summer months due to its proximity to Massachusetts. The village houses the *Seashore Trolley Museum* with its collection of over 100 trolleys from all over the United States and Europe. Part of a visit to this museum includes an exciting and educational ride on some of the restored old trolleys. There is indoor tennis at the *Meadows* and excellent golf at the *Arundel Golf Course*. The *Brick Store Museum* in neighboring Kennebunk has a fine display of items from local history and a carriage collection, as well as items of maritime memorabilia.

THE CAPTAIN LORD MANSION

Corner of Greene and Pleasant Streets, Kennebunkport, ME 04046. 207-967-3141. *Innkeepers*: Jim and Shirley Throumoulos. Open all year.

The Captain Lord Mansion is one of the finest examples of nineteenth-century craftsmanship in current use as an inn in the state of Maine. Built in 1812 by a skilled crew of ships' carpenters idled by the British blockade of the harbor, the mansion is an extremely impressive structure with multiple chimneys and a cupola large enough to hold a group of people. Captain Lord clearly could spend as much as he wished to perfect the details of this three-story gem. The front door with its elaborate leaded glass fanlight opens onto an unusual three-story unsupported elliptical staircase of great strength and grace. The wide board pine floors have been restored to their original warmth and the walls of the mansion's common rooms and guest rooms have been covered with carefully selected reproduction wallpaper. The entire restoration of the mansion was accomplished by a Herculean effort on the part of Jim Throumoulos and his carefully chosen crew of artisans.

The romantic qualities of this grand old home are certain to appeal to those who seek a quiet retreat. Relax in front of a fire in one of the guest rooms with a working fireplace or sit in one of the public rooms or in the cupola room itself and read a good book or gaze at the stars. The inn is a popular place both for those travelers who want to stop over on their way further north and for those who come for a longer stay while visiting the Kennebunkport area. Families with children are welcome but are warned that no special facilities exist at the mansion for the entertainment of children. Guests have country-style breakfast around one large table in the kitchen. No other meals are served. The serene atmosphere overall at the inn makes one feel like a guest in a great village home of yesteryear. *Room Rates*: From $40 to $50 per couple per night. The fifth night is free following four nights at the above rates. No pets permitted. *Driving Instructions*: Take exit 3 from I-95 and follow signs to Kennebunkport's Dock Square. When there, turn right onto Ocean Avenue and proceed to Green Street where you turn left up to the corner of Pleasant Street.

THE CHETWYND HOUSE

Chestnut Street, Kennebunkport, ME 04046. 207-967-2235. *Innkeeper*: Mrs. Susan Knowles Chetwynd. Open all year (guests should be sure to check first).

The Chetwynd is a small guest house built in the middle 1800s by Captain Seavey of Kennebunkport. The blue-shuttered white clapboard house is situated in the heart of Kennebunkport just a few blocks from restaurants, art galleries, and craft shops on Dock Square. Across the street from the Chetwynd is the busy Kennebunk River which empties into the ocean one-half mile away. There are two sandy beaches and the rocks of the breakwater are a wonderful place to sit and watch the parade of fishing boats and graceful sailboats heading for the sea. Another relaxing place is the garden at the Chetwynd. The four guest rooms share two baths. Susan Chetwynd serves a delicious breakfast with melon, strawberries, freshly squeezed orange juice, and—if a guest fancies it—oyster stew! Tea and coffee are available anytime. *Room Rates*: Single rooms, $18; double rooms, $26 to $30, breakfast and beverages included. Off season, $14 to $26. No pets permitted. Children are permitted but not encouraged. *Driving Instructions*: At Dock Square, go two blocks toward the ocean. Newly redecorated.

Monhegan Island, Maine

Monhegan Island is accessible only by ferry from Port Clyde or by private boat. The island is quite unimproved by man, although it does have electricity and a moderate supply of drinking water. Do not expect tourist attractions or entertainment. This is a place to relax and withdraw from the hectic pace of city life or even from the comparatively lively life in the coastal Maine tourist centers. Enjoy nature at its finest here and reacquaint yourself with the sea.

ISLAND INN

Shore Road, Monhegan Island, ME 04852. 207-372-9681. *Innkeepers:* Robert and Mary Burton. Open June 18 to September 18.

Just getting here is half the fun. The drive down from Thomaston to Port Clyde is one of our favorites, and then in the tiny, old-fashioned fishing village of Port Clyde, you must board a ferry for a half-hour ride out to the island. Long a favorite of Andrew Wyeth's, Monhegan Island has loyal devotees who are not put off by the somewhat barren, rocky surroundings.

The Island Inn, perched 40 feet above the island's only harbor and wharf, has 38 rooms, most of which share baths. It was built in 1850, and additions in 1907 and 1927 brought it to its present size with its many dormers and its rooftop cupola. The inn has simple, comfortable furnishings, but its main attraction is clearly the setting. Life on Monhegan is as simple as any life can be, with few vehicles, few telephones, limited electricity, and virtually no entertainment other than that provided by Mother Nature and one's own ingenuity. This is an ideal retreat and an unusual vacation experience. The dining room serves three meals of well-cooked Maine food and is open to the public as well as the guests. *Room Rates:* $21 to $28 per person per night. Neither children nor pets are permitted. *Driving Instructions:* Take Route I-95 to Brunswick, Route 1 to Thomaston, then Route 131 to Port Clyde and the Monhegan Ferry.

Newcastle and Damariscotta, Maine

These towns, often referred to as the "twin cities of Maine" are located near the head of the Damariscotta River at the peninsulas that terminate at Boothbay Harbor, Christmas Cove, and Pemaquid Point. The towns retain many of the original colonial homes in a setting that has come to include modern shopping and other commercial enterprises. There is a public bathing area at the *Pemaquid Beach Park* and a *Fisherman's Museum* at Lighthouse Park. The area has excellent fresh-water fishing for trout, pickerel, perch, small-mouthed bass, and landlocked salmon. Charter boats leave for ocean fishing from several sites in the twin towns as well as further down the peninsula at Boothbay Harbor. The lighthouse at *Lighthouse Park* is frequently photographed and painted. The state park at Pemaquid Beach includes *Fort William and Henry* and the *Round Tower* (1692) as well as the *Pemaquid Restoration*, which is an active archaeological digging site where visitors can see the foundations of several historic buildings recently uncovered.

NEWCASTLE INN

River Road, Newcastle, ME 04553. 207-563-5685. *Innkeeper*: Mrs. Carolyn Mercer. Open all year.

The Newcastle is a comfortable New England inn of indeterminate vintage that has been run as an inn by Mrs. Mercer's family for over 25 years. Staying here is rather like being in a nice home that is perfectly maintained and decorated with comfortable contemporary furnishings, including some reproductions of antiques and some family pieces. The inn was originally a five-room cottage, but in later years this was raised in the air and the larger present inn

constructed below it. Some of the nicest rooms are in this older part, now the upstairs, but since they share a bath they appeal only to those who don't require private bath facilities. Other guest rooms in the main inn as well as in a more recently constructed annex have private baths. The inn is known as a quiet establishment without television or telephones in rooms. It is located on a tidal river in the Pemaquid area with nearby rocky beaches and a particularly fine lighthouse. An extra feature here is the inn's fine doll museum. The only meal served is a buffet-style breakfast to guests only. *Room Rates*: Private bath, $17 to $19; connecting bath, $20 to $24; without bath, $13 to $14. No pets permitted. *Driving Instructions*: The inn is located on River Road off Route 1 in Newcastle, north of Wiscassett.

Spruce Head and Owls Head, Maine (including neighboring Thomaston and Rockland)

The village of Spruce Head is a small island connected by bridge to the St. George peninsula outside of Thomaston. It consists of a summer colony of cottages and a modest year-round population including a number of fishermen and lobstermen who work out of the local harbor. There is a rockbound lobster pound that can be seen from the road through the island. There are several antique shops in the area, as well as one of our favorite bookstores, the *Lobster Lane Bookstore*, which has a great many used books and magazines.

Owls Head is a favorite summer vacation spot, with many full summer residents as well as the weekly rental and transient trade. The *Owls Head Lighthouse* is one of Maine's most beautiful. Across from the tiny general store in Owls Head is a wonderful antique store crammed to the ceilings (literally) with antiques, memorabilia, and junk, all of which has spilled into the shop's front yard, making this a wonderful place to browse on an otherwise gloomy day.

Rockland is a small city best known for its *Seafood Festival* held the first weekend in August each year. Tons of lobster, shrimp, and french fries are consumed annually at this fest. The

Farnsworth Library and Art Museum has an unusually good collection of nineteenth- and twentieth-century art including some works by Wyeth and other Maine artists.

Thomaston has some of the most prestigious homes in mid-coast Maine lining its Main Street. It is the home of *"Montpelier,"* the reconstruction of General Knox's mansion, now open as a museum during the summer months. The Maine State Prison is here and trusted inmates under supervision operate a *Prison Workshop Store* with a variety of well-made wooden furniture in the front and an inmates' craft gallery in the rear. Inmates will be happy to answer questions about the products in the shop. Some crafts are crude and charming, while others, especially some scale model ships, show the incredible skill and patience of the workers.

For further information on this general area, see also the section on Tenants Harbor.

CRAIGNAIR INN

Clark Island Road, St. George, ME. Mailing address: Spruce Head, ME 04859. 207-594-7644. *Innkeepers:* Terry Smith and Norman Smith. Open from April to November.

Craignair is an unpretentious seaside country inn. Dotted with islands, the coastline in this part of Maine is very picturesque and removed from the bustle of the more populous resort areas.

Originally built to house granite quarry workers, Craignair is located at the end of the road that leads to Clark Island. (Ospreys nest on the disused quarry poles.) The plain, white, unshuttered

building has 16 guest rooms; most share hall baths. Set above the ocean and Clark Island as well as the local cove, the dining room and many of the guest rooms have an unobstructed view of the sea. A deck on the seaside allows guests to relax in the sun while watching the lobster boats at work and, closer to shore, the sea gulls and other local shore birds. This is not an inn with fancy surroundings or a myriad of resort-style activities. It is likely to appeal to writers, naturalists, artists, beachcombers, and anyone seeking relaxation and an opportunity to reaffirm one's inherent connection with the sea. *Room Rates*: July and August, $24 per person, MAP. May, June, September, and October, $22 per person, MAP. Weekly rates available as are EP accommodations. Pets are permitted. *Driving Instructions*: From Route 1, just east of Thomaston, take Route 131 south 5½ miles to Route 73, then left 1 mile to Clark Island Road. Turn right on Clark Island Road and the inn will be 1½ miles ahead.

Tenants Harbor, Maine

Tenants Harbor is a small lobstering village with a modest summer tourist population. Its seclusion on the peninsula running from Thomaston to Port Clyde has meant that its New England character has remained generally unchanged. It is one of seven villages within the township of St. George and was settled in 1605. The village area was once a major source of granite. Its inhabitants also supported themselves by fishing and lobstering. For many years, the village was a major shipbuilding center, and many large vessels were built in Tenants Harbor. At low tide several wrecks can still be seen here. Day trips to Port Clyde (and from there by ferry to Monhegan Island) and to the neighboring communities of Spruce Head, St. George, South Thomaston, Thomaston, Owls Head, and Rockland provide the visitor to this area with a taste of the same fine scenery and seafaring life that inspired so many of Andrew Wyeth's paintings when he lived nearby.

THE EAST WIND

Tenants Harbor, ME 04860. 207-372-8800 or 372-8908. *Inn-keepers*: Tim Watts and Ginnie Wheeler. Open all year.

Snuggled in a corner of the peaceful village of Tenant's Harbor is the East Wind, built in 1890 and restored in 1975. The inn is within walking distance of the village library and post office and a short drive from all the attractions on the St. George Peninsula, stretching from Thomaston to Port Clyde. The inn was built as a sail loft and ship chandler's operation. The gracious old white frame structure has 16 guest rooms, 2 with private baths. The first floor contains a large kitchen, pantries, a dining room that over-looks the harbor, a spacious lobby, office, and manager's room. The rooms are simply decorated with wall-to-wall carpeting throughout, and many antiques including brass beds. Three meals are served daily to guests. Dinners feature seafood including lob-ster prepared three ways, haddock, clams, scallops, and a shore dinner, with steaks and chicken Kiev for those who don't care for seafood. Prices for full dinners range from $3.95 to $15.95 (for the shore dinner); most with seafood and steak cost $5.95 to $7.95.

There are no traffic jams, no noise, no pollution, and no fast-food restaurants here. There is, instead, fresh sea air, four-season recre-ation, and congenial hosts at one of Maine's newest old inns. *Room Rates*: From June through September, rates range from $18 for a single room to $36 for a two-room suite. Off season rates are $6 to $8 less. *Driving Instructions*: From U.S. 1, just east of Thomaston, take Route 131 south 9.5 miles to Tenant's Harbor, then turn left at the post office and continue straight to the inn.

√ Wiscasset, Maine

As you drive north through Wiscasset on Route 1 and you have left the central village, look to the right at the harbor and you will see one of the most eerie and yet romantic sights of coastal Maine. There, at the shoreline, lie the remains of two grand old schooners. Grey, shadowy reminders of the glory of sailing days gone by, these majestic giants are now lying on their sides, slowly being reclaimed by the sea they once sailed.

Wiscasset is a much visited and photographed coastal village. There are many antique and craft shops here and several small, pleasant restaurants. Among the museums in the area are the *Lincoln County Fire Museum* with its collection of antique fire trucks, hearses, and carriages; the *Lincoln County Museum* and old *Lincoln County Jail*; the *Maine Art Gallery* with its collection of work by Maine artists including art for sale; and, finally, the *Music Museum*, displaying a wide variety of old musical instruments.

THE SQUIRE TARBOX INN

Westport Island, ME. Mailing Address: RFD 2, Box 318, Wiscasset, ME 04578. 207-882-7693. *Innkeepers*: Elsie White and Anne McInvale. Closed during the winter.

The Squire Tarbox is a rare find in Maine—an old country inn in an incomparable setting. It is located on a 10-mile-long island near Wiscasset, linked to the mainland by bridge. Westport Island has one main road, Route 144, running the length of it. At the end of this road is an old house, part of it dating from 1793. The larger main building was added later. Today the property consists of a main house and a barn with connecting smaller sections between. In this way, the farmer and his family were able to walk from their

house to the barn to do chores without the necessity of going out into the bitter cold winter weather.

The house was carefully restored some years ago and it retains the original floors, carvings, moldings, fireplaces, wainscotting, and old glass windows so characteristic of a home of the early nineteenth century. This is not a large inn; the seven guest rooms are almost always occupied. Each summer, guests are drawn here by the crisp, clean Maine air. This is a place for people who love old things and do not require the organized activity of larger inns or resorts.

The Squire Tarbox recently changed ownership. Continental breakfast is served, but other meals are optional. We do not know anything about their meals except that, in most cases, there is a single sitting for dinner and that advance reservations are necessary. *Room Rates*: Single rooms, $20; double rooms, $30; both include continental breakfast. There is a charge of $5 for each additional occupant in a room. *Driving Instructions*: Take Route 1 north of Bath. Just before entering the village of Wiscasset, take Route 144 to the right and cross onto Westport Island; then continue to the inn.

York, Maine

York, first settled in 1630, is the second southernmost village in Maine. It has the distinction of having 10 particularly fine old colonial houses that have been fully restored and are open to the public on their original sites. For this reason, York has described itself as a "living Colonial Museum." The town is perhaps the nation's finest historic "preservation" as contrasted to reassembled "historic restorations or reconstructions." Among the houses open to the public (some for a small fee) are the *Old Gaol Museum* with its dungeons and other prison accouterments; the *Emerson-Wilcox House*; the *1745 School House* (listed on the National Register of Historic Houses); the *G. A. Marshall Country Store*, currently housing a fine sample of contemporary crafts fashioned by area artisans; and the *John Hancock Warehouse*, a restored colonial commercial building once owned by the signer of the Declaration, currently housing a collection of antique tools and ship models.

DOCKSIDE GUEST QUARTERS

Harris Island Road, York, ME 03909. 207-363-2868. *Innkeeper*: David Lusty. Open Memorial Day through Columbus Day.

The Guest Quarters is located on an eight-acre private peninsula that becomes an island at high tide. Access is from Route 103 in York. Much of this island has been developed by Mr. Lusty, who has constructed several modern cottage units that provide some accommodations. However, the "Maine House" is the original dwelling on the island. It is an 18-room, 3-story white clapboard New England guest house. This structure was fully resored when Mr. Lusty purchased the island and is currently decorated with antiques. Rooms in the Maine House have an "old inn" feeling, while the new cottages have the look and feel of modern motel units. All but two of the rooms in the various buildings have private baths. There is also a new restaurant as well as a marina. The spacious grounds boast swings and a treehouse to entertain children. The overall feeling at Harris Island is a mixture of the old-fashioned and contemporary, but it is altogether very comfortable. The restaurant serves three meals daily, with lunch and dinner available to the general public. House specialties include roast duckling and lobster, with dinner prices ranging from $5.50 to $8.95. The restaurant is a contemporary structure with attached deck for dining outdoors in warm weather. *Room Rates*: From mid-June to mid-September, from $19 to $31 for twin and double rooms, with apartment suites from $37 to $44.50. Off season rates are 15 percent lower. *Driving Instructions*: Take I-95 to the York exit and then take Route 1A to Maine Route 103. Follow Route 103 to Harris Island Road, watching for the signs to the inn.

INLAND

Bethel, Maine

Bethel is a lumbering and farming center located along the Androscoggin and Sunday Rivers in the Oxford Hills, adjacent to the foothills of the White Mountains and within a short distance of the immense *White Mountain National Forest*, a portion of which lies within the state of Maine. The combination of the area's rolling hills and the backdrop of the White Mountains provides some of Maine's most memorable interior scenery. Visitors to Bethel in the winter can enjoy downhill skiing at the *Sunday River Skiway* and at *Mount Abram* and cross-country skiing at the *Sunday River Inn* and along trails in the *White Mountain National Forest.*

The grandeur of the mountains is no less evident in the summer, when hiking along well-marked forest trails and shopping for antiques and crafts take over as leisurely activities. Bethel also has a covered bridge over the Sunday River.

SUNDAY RIVER INN

Sunday River Skiway Access Road, Bethel, ME 04217. Mailing Address: RFD 2, Box 141, Bethel, ME 04217. 207-824-2410. *Innkeepers*: Steve and Peggy Wight. Open October to May.

The Sunday River is not an old country inn. It is included here, however, because it is a small, family-oriented inn with a special devotion to skiers in an area that has relatively few inns of any sort. Furthermore, the inn is run by a young couple determined to allow their guests to take full advantage of the area's resources.

The Sunday River Inn is located at the edge of a large tract of wilderness managed for timber production by paper companies and private tree farmers. The inn operates the Sunday River Ski Touring Center on the premises with its 25 miles of groomed and maintained trails and hundreds of miles of unmarked logging roads. Equipment and instruction are available, as are a waxing and warming room, guided tours, and night skiing lit by kerosine lamps

on Friday nights. The Outward Bound School uses the inn as the lunch base for its winter program.

The inn itself is a simple building with the ski shop in an attached small barn. Built in 1965—and given later improvements—the inn has inviting stone fireplaces in both the living and dining rooms. There are 12 guest rooms, none with private baths. In addition to the guest rooms, two sleeping-bag bunk dorm-rooms are popular with teenage members of families. Meals too are simple here, with only one entree served family style. Typical meals include roast beef, turkey, or meat loaf. *Room Rates*: Double rooms, $19 per person, MAP; bunk rooms, $14 per person, MAP (bring your own sleeping bag). No pets permitted. *Driving Instructions*: Take Route 2 east from Bethel for two miles. Turn left at the sign for the Sunday River Ski Area; then go three miles to the inn.

THE SUDBURY INN

Main Street, Bethel, ME 04217. 207-824-2174. *Innkeepers*: Douglas and Sharon Scott. Open all year.

First open to the public in 1873, this inn was initially an overnight stopping place for nineteenth-century businessmen. Now it serves tourists who visit the area in all four seasons, especially since travelers have discovered that inland Maine offers fine winter sports with fewer crowds than in neighboring New Hampshire and Vermont. The inn offers accommodations in 16 rooms, 3 with private baths. Rooms are generally large, with solid country furniture very much in keeping with a nineteenth-century inn that appeals

to twentieth-century tastes. The inn's restaurant serves three meals daily to guests and the public and is particularly proud of its scallops Newberg, lamb shashlik, and chicken orange. The "Ploughman's Rest" lounge has a fireplace and copper bar, and there is a large lobby with plenty of good reading material and comfortable chairs for those who want to read quietly after a day on the ski slopes or hiking through the forest. *Room Rates*: Double rooms, from $15 to $22 depending on bath location. Pets are permitted. *Driving Instructions*: The inn is on Main Street, one block south of Route 26 in Bethel.

Greenville, Maine (Moosehead Lake Region)

The greater Moosehead Lake region is a true wilderness. Maine's North Woods have a pervasive atmosphere and a history of logging. The area away from the lake is owned by giant paper companies, and logging is still very much in evidence. The woods and the water are open to everyone. This is the country of Henry David Thoreau, who described it in detail in *The Maine Woods*, based upon his travels in the area in the mid-1800's. At that time this was Indian land, but control later passed to industry.

Moosehead is the largest lake in Maine. It is about 40 miles long and 20 miles wide at its widest point. Here you can see not only the moose for which the lake was named, but deer, bear, and a multitude of smaller mammals, as well as numerous game and other birds. The Moosehead Lake region boasts over 200 miles of groomed snowmobile trails and the *Squaw Mountain Ski Area*, a ski resort for all ages which emphasizes family winter vacations. This is a great region for hunting and fishing, with many sports lovers flying in to their preferred sections by seaplane. There are several outfitters who rent boats and canoes and will supply guides for trips to the more remote sections. Canoers who plan to explore without a guide should beware of sudden squalls and high winds.

WILSON'S ON MOOSEHEAD LAKE

Route 15, Moosehead Lake, East Outlet, ME. Mailing Address: Star Route 84, Greenville Junction, ME 04442. 207-695-2549. *Innkeepers*: Ron and Jane Fowler. Open all year.

Wilson's consists of a group of 15 housekeeping cottages which sleep up to 18 people, grouped around an old colonial house with an interesting history. The original house was built prior to 1865 by Henry Wilson, a dam keeper on Moosehead Lake. He was asked to be the dam keeper at East Outlet and he agreed on the condition that he be allowed to bring his house with him. The old house was then floated across the lake and placed on the shore at East Outlet. Later, an inn and a water tower were attached to the original Wilson house. The result is a rather unique assemblage of buildings with many floors, passages, and stairways to wander through and explore. The old "hotel" is now used as a combination office room, recreation building, and general attraction for the cottages. Guests are welcome to explore it.

Most of the cottages are log cabins, all with housekeeping facilities, furnished with pieces from the hotel and newer furniture. Many have fireplaces. The inn has its own beach, dock, boats, and canoes (there are additional charges for use of boats and canoes). There is fine fishing in the lake or in the Kennebec River, which begins at the end of the cabins. This is a year-round place and many visitors come in the winter for skiing and snowmobiling. *Room Rates*: From $18 to $50 (for the 18-person lodge) a day, with $25 a typical figure for a cabin that sleeps four and has a fireplace. Weekly charges for this cabin would be about $145. Pets are permitted. *Driving Instructions*: Take the Maine Turnpike to the Newport exit, Route 17 to Corinna. Then take Route 7 to Dexter and Route 23 to Guilford. Take Route 15 to Greenville, six miles past Squaw Mountain.

FROST POND CAMPS AND CAMPGROUND

Star Route 76, Frost Pond, Greenville, ME 04441. Telephone: Two-way radio contact with Folsom's Air Service in Greenville. Messages may be left with Folsom's by calling 207-695-2821 before 4:00 P.M. Seven days a week. *Innkeepers*: Eric and Judith Givens. Cabins are available May 15 through November 30 and in winter months with advance notice. After December 15, access is by ski or snowmobile.

Frost Pond is so wonderful and remote (40 miles from the nearest town, Millinocket) that we had to include it. Frost Pond Camps are best described as rustic, and that is their attraction. It is a comfortable but rugged wilderness camp on a quiet lake surrounded by forests of spruce, fir, maple, birch, and beech. There are eight cabins equipped with gas stoves, refrigerators, electric lights, and wood stoves. Seven others have no electricity or water, but water may be obtained from the well. The one larger cabin has hot and cold running water, shower, and indoor toilet. The cabins accommodate from two to eight people. Frost Pond is a brook trout haven, squaretails over 1½ pounds are not uncommon, and the Givens have seen some weighing close to 4 pounds. Boats, canoes, and outboards are available for rent or you can launch your own. The North Woods teem with wildlife—moose, bear, fox, and snowshoe hare, to name a few. It's a bird lover's paradise with great horned owls, bald eagles, ducks of all sorts, loons, and many species of warblers and finches. The 200,000-acre *Baxter State Park* 15 miles away offers a variety of trails for hiking and mountain climbing. Mount Katahdin, Maine's highest peak (5267 feet), is located in the park and is visible from Frost Pond.

If guests wish to eat out there are restaurants in Millinocket (40 miles away) and Greenville (50 miles away). *Cabin Rates*: The rates vary according to length of stay, ranging from $5 to $8 a day per person. *Camp sites*: $3 a day or $16 a week. Pets are permitted. *Driving Instructions*: Take I-95 north to Medway exit, then take Route 157 west to Millinocket. Follow Baxter State Park road northwest past park entrance to its junction with Great Northern Paper Company Road. Follow this road to Ripogenus Dam (drive carefully; the road is heavily used by trucks hauling tree-length logs). The camp is three miles beyond.

Moose River-Jackman area (Maine's north woods)

Located deep in Maine's north country—not far from the Canadian border—are the towns of Moose River and Jackman. The area is northeast of Moosehead Lake, Maine's largest lake and one of the most beautiful in the east. The two towns are situated on the Moose River, with the border mountains rising around them and scores of lakes and streams filled with landlocked salmon and trout. This is perfect terrain for cross-country skiing on abandoned logging trails, hiking, and hunting. There is also excellent fishing, boating, and canoeing in the area. Fly-in trips can be arranged in

Greenville and at other airports. Jackman has seaplane facilities; Moose River has an airport at Sky Lodge. Boats and canoes can be rented in the towns. Guides are recommended for treks into the remote areas around the towns; arrangements can be made through the lodges and in towns. It is generally dangerous to attempt extended trips into the wilderness without guides. This applies to canoers—there are many white-water areas and falls as well as wooded portages. There are lodges and fishing camps in the towns and the surrounding area for a real wilderness vacation any time of the year.

SKY LODGE AND MOTEL

Route 201, Moose River, ME 04945. Mailing address: Jackman, Maine 04945. 207-668-2171. *Innkeeper*: E. R. Landgraf. Open from May 28 through November 22.

Sky Lodge is the largest all-log lodge in the northeast. Built in 1929 on the spot where the original settlers of the Jackman-Moose River area built their homes, the rustic lodge sits high on a clearing in the remote, unspoiled north woods, surrounded by the breathtaking panorama of the Maine border mountains, lakes, and pine forests. The 200 acres offer a world of outdoor activities— hiking and exploring the pine woods and lakes—and near the lodge shuffleboard, archery, horseshoes, badminton, and also swimming in the pool. A golf course is adjacent to the lodge grounds; boating, canoeing, and fishing in the remote Maine waters are all within one mile. The main room of the inn is a big, two-storied affair with two enormous stone fireplaces and curving stairs leading up to the bearskin rug-draped balcony and the guest rooms. These rooms are all furnished with handmade pine furniture and "snowshoe" chairs (snowshoe furniture can be purchased in the gift shop). The 11 guest rooms in the lodge and 14 in the motel down the hill all have private baths. Six of the lodge's guest rooms have working stone fireplaces—one even has a fireplace in the bathroom. The Sky Lodge dining room is open to the public for all three meals. The large picture windows offer a spectacular view of the countryside. Good, hearty American food is featured and the menu is changed daily. On a typical evening one could have a Swiss cheese omelet, grilled pork chops with Dutch apples, Maine lobster, or a fresh, poached salmon in egg sauce. The freshly baked breads and homemade desserts are plentiful. There is also a congenial cocktail lounge complete with one of the giant stone fireplaces. For pilots, there is a fine 1750-foot grass strip and 80/87 octane fuel is available at the lodge's airport. *Room Rates*: Current rates were not available at the time of publication. Reservations are advisable. Pets permitted at the lodge's discretion. *Driving and Flying Instructions*: Driving—Route 201, two miles north of Jackman. Flying—Sky Lodge Airport is on the Lewiston sectional aeronautical chart.

Sebago Lake area, Maine (including Casco, South Casco, Long Lake, and Bridgeton)

Sebago Lake is second only to Moosehead Lake in size within the state of Maine. It is an extremely popular lake for summer visitors who are drawn by its fine salmon fishing in early summer and fall and by its trout and bass fishing in the warmer months. Water sports are popular here as are guided or nonguided fishing trips, which often go the entire length of the lake and pass through the Songo River Locks at the northwestern end. Tourists then have access to Long Lake, which is an additional 20 miles or more long, making the double lake system of about 40 miles of open water.

Bridgeton, on Long Lake, is one of the largest antique centers in the state, with more than 25 active dealers. Bridgeton is best known as a tourist center due to its lakeside location, its own golf course and tennis courts at the *Bridgeton Highlands Country Club*, and its public swimming areas on the lake. The annual bike race around Long Lake takes place in mid-August. There is an art show each Columbus Day weekend which is open to artists working in all media. The Bridgeton Historical Society operates a small museum. These towns are a short drive from *Pleasant Mountain* with its ski area, the second largest in Maine. There are a hanggliding school and a summer chair lift at Pleasant Mountain.

South Casco is the home of the Marsh House, built in 1780, and of an old windmill. The State of Maine Fish Hatchery at Casco is open to the public and offers explanations of the fish-stocking program within the state.

MIGIS LODGE

South Casco, ME 04077. 207-655-4524. *Innkeeper*: Gene P. Porta. Open from May 25 to October 10.

There are few true "country inns" around the lakes of Maine, and Migis Lodge is no exception. But it is a well-run lodge with guest rooms in about 25 surrounding cottages. Set on Lake Sebago, the largest in southern Maine, the lodge offers overnight accommodations in the cottages, with daily maid service and a cabin boy (to handle luggage and firewood), but all meals are served in the Main Lodge. The cottages are heated and have wood-burning fireplaces. The furnishings are a mixture of modern and colonial with wood paneling in most rooms. The Main Lodge has the dining room, the living room, offices, and a library. The lodge provides many recreational activities for its guests, including swimming at the lakefront, sailing, water-skiing, canoeing, and fishing from one of a fleet of aluminum motor boats. The lake is known for its excellent landlocked salmon fishing (the best months are May, June, and September), as well as fishing for bass and trout. The lodge recreation hall provides bingo, movies, talent shows, magic shows, pool, and bumper pool. There is also outdoor shuffleboard. *Room Rates*: $32 to $38 per person, AP. No pets permitted. *Driving Instructions*: Take I-95 to the Maine Turnpike. Exit 8 from the turnpike and follow Route 302 for 20 miles to South Casco.

The Forks, Maine

The Forks is a sparsely populated area of northwestern Maine along Route 201. This highway runs from Waterville toward Quebec and was the route used by Benedict Arnold and his men for their assault on that fortress city during the Revolutionary War. The road is absolutely spectacular, with great vistas at every turn. The area has fine canoeing, snowmobiling, hunting, fishing, and cross-country skiing. Guides are available through local innkeepers or town offices.

CRAB APPLE ACRES

Route 201, The Forks, ME. Mailing address: West Forks, ME 04985. 207-663-2218. *Innkeeper*: Eleanore Evans. Open all year.

Crab Apple Acres is a small, white clapboard farmhouse in a rather remote section of Somerset County. The farm offers seven guest rooms, which share two baths. It is popular with people seeking a peaceful retreat, and with hunters, snowmobilers, and those on canoe trips. The farmhouse has many old-fashioned features, including the original fanlight over the door, Dutch-oven fireplace, wide floor boards, original Christian-cross doors, and old hinges and thumb latches. Meals are family style, mostly to guests, but the public is welcome by reservation. Mrs. Evans takes great pride in the home-style food served.

In mid-August there are the annual white-water canoe races on Dead River and the bicycle race from Jackman to Waterville. Winter activities include snowmobiling and cross-country skiing (on unmarked trails). The nearest formal recreational facilities are at least 25 miles away, so this farm is definitely for those content to enjoy the entertainment provided by the natural setting itself. *Room Rates*: $14 to $16 per person, AP. *Driving Instructions*: Take Route I-95 to the Skowhegan, Quebec exit and then take Route 201 to the farmhouse in The Forks.